BRINGING DREAMS TO LIFE

Learning to Interpret Your Dreams

GEORGE R. SLATER, PH.D.

PAULIST PRESS
New York • Mahwah, N.J.

Limited Permission to Photocopy

The "Worksheet for Dream Analysis" which appears in the back of this book may be photocopied or otherwise duplicated for use by individuals. However, this copyrighted work may not be published or be distributed among groups of people without permission from the publisher.

The diagram of the "Ego-Self Axis" is reprinted from *Ego and Archetype* by Edward Edinger, © 1972 by the C.G. Jung Foundation for Analytical Psychology, by arrangement with Shambala Publications, Inc. P.O. Box 308, Boston MA 02117.

Library of Congress Cataloging-in-Publication Data

    Slater, George R.
    Bringing dreams to life :   learning to interpret your dreams/ George R. Slater.
       p. cm.
    Includes bibliographical references and index.
    ISBN 0-8091-3568-X (alk. paper)
    1. Dream interpretation. 2. Dreams. 3. Symbolism (Psychology)
4. Psychoanalysis. I. Title.
BF175.5.D74S53   1995
154.6'34—dc20

                        95-3246
                          CIP

Published by Paulist Press
997 Macarthur Boulevard
Mahwah, New Jersey 07430

Printed and bound in the
United States of America

CONTENTS

iv   *Contents*

We know not a voice of that River,

If vocal or silent it be,

Where forever and ever and ever

It flows to no sea.

More deep than the seas is that River,

More full than their manifold tides,

Where forever and ever and ever

It flows and abides, abides.

—Christina Rossetti

INTRODUCTION

Fascination with dreams, like the glint of a nugget in a prospector's pan, awakens a widespread and enthusiastic response. Only a few, however, go on to the actual discipline of mining their dreams for the gold that is there. There's a heavy price to be paid in the time to record and work on their dreams, and, if they choose help, a considerable investment of time and money for analysis.

For those who want to understand their dreams better, but who don't want to go into analysis, there is a growing body of books about dreams and dream symbols, about the role of the unconscious in giving messages for personal growth, and dictionaries of symbols to suggest possible meanings. The subject of dream interpretation, however, is so complex that it is overwhelming to the average person. Attempts to simplify matters, as some guides do, by offering pat, one-dimensional meanings for symbols, for example, can be misleading, even dangerous. Many of the books that approach the subject in a reliable way tend to focus on the theoretical level, leaving the beginner at sea so far as a practical method of analysis is concerned.

It is to meet this need that this book is offered. In what follows I want to provide a simple but reliable format with suggested techniques to use in analyzing one's own dreams, or in working with the help of a partner. My purpose is to give ordinary people a way of understanding their dreams and thereby enriching their lives. In the process, I hope to demonstrate how real is that hidden part of ourselves from which dreams come and

1

how relevant the wisdom of the dream can be to specific
life situations.

To speak of dreams as life enriching raises the question
of how this level of dream interpretation may be related to
therapy. Although this book claims only to be an intro-
duction to dreams and their interpretation, any attempt to
analyze dreams lands us squarely in the process of what I
would prefer to call spiritual transformation. Carl Jung, the
pioneer Swiss psychoanalyst, spoke of "individuation," of
growing to fulfil one's unique destiny by bringing all that
the unconscious will give into the business of conscious
living. Dreaming is like fishing: it brings us in touch with
what lies hidden in the depths and brings it up for human
need. Fishing is as old as humanity, and through the ages
we have used net, spear or hook to catch the life that
teems in the depths. So fishing has become a symbol for
finding soul-food or even one's soul. In one way or
another, all of us are like fishermen seeking to deal with
the fact that our stomachs are empty and our lives
incomplete. Before us is the great river or sea. Beneath its
surface, we glimpse occasional flickers of silver bellies
and sense the dark movement of life in the depths. But it is
a whole other world and needs a very special skill to
access. Dreaming is a kind of nightly fishing expedition.
From out of the unconscious, it lands the images and
symbols that enlighten, guide and fulfill our conscious
lives and may help move us forward on the journey to
wholeness. So, when we speak of how dreams can enrich
life, we mean much more than merely understanding an
interesting dream image: dreams can be life-changing and
healing.

For the most part, I choose to follow the psychological
understanding of dreams and their source in the
unconscious developed by Jung who, along with Sigmund

Freud, pioneered the interpretation of dreams early in this century. In order to use the techniques and format that follow, however, it is not necessary for the reader to have any previous knowledge of psychology. The worksheet format for dream interpretation which is presented here develops in a step-by-step progression that is explained as you go. It provides a practical means of analyzing your dreams and presents techniques for opening up the meaning of images and symbols.

Beyond learning a format for analyzing their dreams, some may have related questions, such as, how dreams are structured, how they work as part of a person's psychological system, what practical value they might have, and how their meanings may be applied beneficially to one's life. To go into these matters requires that we go further and look into a theory of dreams. Here it is helpful to grasp a basic Jungian understanding of how dreams function in giving meaning to consciousness and healing to the whole psyche. I have attempted a very rudimentary theoretical outline for that purpose which is written assuming no previous acquaintance with Jung or analysis. This follows the presentation of the worksheet format of dream analysis in chapter 7.

What follows has grown out of numerous dream workshops, courses and seminars I have given over the past fourteen years and from twenty years of keeping track of my own dreams. It also depends heavily on my work with analysands. I want to thank these analysands, students and workshop participants for sharing their dreams, and themselves, with such patience and commitment. Their humanity has been an inspiring teacher for me. In making reference to their dreams, I have altered details to preserve anonymity. All dreams are used with the permission of the dreamer, but some dreams have been edited and, as a result, some dreamers may not fully recognize their dream or its interpretation.

Analysis is the best teacher of analysis. The most powerful influences shaping my understanding of dream interpretation were my analysis with the late Fraser Boa and my work with Marion Woodman, though I in no way hold them responsible for any errors or distortions that may appear in the following. I am deeply grateful to them both. I am also grateful to those who have assisted with criticism, support and encouragement. In addition to my wife, Glenda, and my family, I want to recognize especially Steve Fisher, Margaret Brillinger, Leonard Griffith and Vickie Grant for their help.

In this book I want to honor the concept of inclusive language. However, it can become cumbersome to repeat references in order to give equal gender recognition. Therefore, I have chosen to alternate the use of personal pronouns at random throughout the text to convey the sense of mutual gender identification.

The Experience of Dreams

1
THE DREAM PHENOMENON

"I had a strange dream last night." Those words are likely spoken thousands of times each morning, all over the world, in hundreds of languages, by young and old, educated and uneducated. They might have been said to others on rising, or over breakfast; or spoken internally to oneself to acknowledge an important awareness before the day swept it away. Whatever the unique details, we are pulled back to the memory of something mysterious that happened in our sleep.

Most of us have this experience of dreaming. Sometime during sleep, we enter a state that is not sleep at all, but a time and a place quite its own. Something unfolds on the screen of our mind like our own private video. We know we are somehow a part of it or it is "ours," but we have little or no control over it. We may dismiss it as irrelevant, shake our head in puzzlement, wonder at its power and beauty or shrink from it in terror, but, having dreamed, we have to admit it is a real part of our experience. Dreams are facts of our life. Even if we forget what we dreamed, most of us know that we have dreamed. But what is this dream experience? And how are we to understand it?

What do you experience when you dream?

A Different World

When we dream we enter a world that is different than the everyday world. In dreams, fairytale-like things

7

happen: monsters materialize in the park at the corner; kings, queens and princesses hold court; knights gallop by in full armor; and talking toads stare at us. A space odyssey may unfold and we are gripped in a battle of the galaxies, or a hydrogen bomb may explode in our last dream of the night. People may possess fantastic abilities or do diabolical deeds; objects may transform into animals, elevators become subway cars, time may shrink or expand and laws of normal cause and effect may be suspended.

One man told me of a flying dream. He was canoeing with his wife on a large bay far from land and sensed that a storm was coming up and they might not make it safely to land. So he put out his arms like wings and began to fly. Up over the water he went and surveyed the whole area including the island and its dock which was their destination. Then he flew back toward the canoe again. In waking life he was a very rational human being. He could only laugh with amusement and amazement at the wonderfully different world of dreams.

The strange and fantastic may equally take the form of terrifying nightmares, beings that threaten you, circumstances that overwhelm you. How often people will report that they woke up just as they were about to be caught by a villain or as some disastrous outcome was to befall them.

In the majority of cases, dreams may be different from waking reality not because they represent extraordinary powers, harmful or otherwise, but simply because they give an altered view from that which we usually hold. It is as if the point of the dream is to show how different the dream outlook is from our outlook when awake. For example, a business executive returned from his vacation to tell me that he had taken up the guitar and was rediscovering the joy of music. As he began to develop his musical skills, he had the following dream:

> I am in Florence, Italy, and go with another man to a business meeting. As I look down, I see my fingers all cut off halfway down. I realize that this is somehow the result of doing business.

Reflecting on the dream, he told me he loved Italy and saw himself as a Renaissance man, creative and many-talented. The image of the half-cut-off fingers leaped out at him. His fingers represented his new-found creativity which was in danger of being cut off by business pressures. Until then, he had not recognized that the demands of his work were in conflict with his artistic expression. There was the altered reality. He now knew that in order to keep his free, expansive creativity alive, a workaholic, like himself, must not let work tyrannize him.

A Real Experience

Having said that dreams are different than waking reality, I want also to say that in most dreams you have the sense that what you are experiencing is absolutely real. It is so real, sometimes, that you will kick or cry out in your sleep and wake up with sweaty palms and your heart racing. Your body knows that you have actually been living the dream. Sleep studies show that the body's physical responses during a dream are almost identical to the actual activity represented in the dream.

Dreaming can seem so real that a dreamer may feel that what takes place in the dream has actually happened. A man who lived through the Second World War as a boy in Europe told of the frequent food shortages and scant meals they endured. In the midst of a particularly lean time he had a dream in which he saw jars of cooking oil hidden in his backyard. They were so clear he could read the printing on the labels. The image of the gold margin around the label and its black lettering stood out vividly. When he awakened, the sense of the dream was so real that he went out into the yard behind his house fully expecting to find those jars of oil. When he told me his dream, he could still see the image of the label clearly and read the exact words, though it was more than fifty years later.

A Story or Drama

Most dreams take the form of a story or an unfolding drama, like a play with characters, a plot, a climax and denouement. In fact, some dreams may actually be set on a stage with characters playing out their roles. Sometimes the dreamer is one of the actors, sometimes an observer in the audience.

One woman told me that as a young girl her dreams had been like extended stories which continued to unfold night after night. In her waking life at the time she would read novels to avoid boredom. Dreaming for this young girl was like opening a novel every night after she had gone to sleep. In time, she came to look forward to the next episode. It was a form of entertainment for her.

Recurrent Dreams

Often people experience the same dream repeated over and over again over a period of months or years. It is often puzzling to them why the same dream should recur. One person said her recurring dream was frightening: "For over a year I kept dreaming of running down a long hallway which only had closed doors on each side, and I kept knocking to see if any door would open." Always there was the same sense of frantic search and always the frustration that no door would open to her.

Rather than repeat the identical scene, the dream may repeat the same general theme. "I'm always flying in my dreams," said one workshop participant. "It's a wonderful sense of freedom." Another person said, "I'm always running in my dreams. Someone's chasing me, but I can never see who it is."

Frequently the repeating factor may be some task the dreamer is never able to complete successfully, or a goal that continues to elude the person. Like Tantalus in the Greek fable, whose burden would slide down again every time he managed to push it up, so some people dream of a persistently frustrating circumstance that they seem never to be able to overcome—like being chased by a villain or monster and always slipping in the mud or having your feet taken out from under you and falling down just when you need to run or stand firm.

The repeating factor may be the same type of setting where the action of the dream takes place. Doctors may dream frequently of operating rooms or patients, teachers of classrooms and students, perhaps because those settings are the context for much of their daily living and are the sphere of their emotional life. Before entering private practice as a psychotherapist, I served as a minister in several congregations. Even after fifteen years' absence from active church work, many of my dreams continue to be set in pastoral settings. Some people dream of the same few people. Others have exotic travel places as their recurrent factor, travelling to the orient, for example. I know a Canadian who frequently dreams of travelling to the United States. Another common repeating dream is to be in a maze.

Déjà Vu Dreams

There are dreams which point forward and seem to anticipate a future event or dreams which depend on a future event to provide a clue to their meaning. When that event happens the dream may seem as if we had been there before. These are sometimes called "precognitive dreams" and have the sense of "déjà vu" (literally, already seen). A man told me the following dream, which illustrates this kind of occurrence:

> I dream of a male figure, with a deformed left arm, sitting cross-legged. It is a rather large person. Then the dream shifts and I see a web-like sack containing a squirming creature of some kind. I can't make out what kind of animal or being it is, but it seems heavy.

At the time the dream made no sense whatever to him, but four days later, in a chance meeting, he was speaking with his aunt who, in a totally different context and without any knowledge of his dream, mentioned that his mother often sat cross-legged. Furthermore, she, the aunt, could remember his mother sitting that way on a couch when she had been pregnant with the dreamer. All of this came out spontaneously, unprompted and certainly unimagined by the dreamer.

The connection hit the man almost physically: he realized that the web-like sack and its squirming creature represented him in his mother's womb. It struck him as odd that he would be in conversation with that aunt, and odder still that such a bizarre reference to his mother would be made. But strangest of all was this repetition of the image from his dream four days earlier. Without the accidental meeting and chance comment of the aunt, he would not likely have been able to make that connection. It still left unanswered the question why the figure in his dream was male and had a deformed left arm.

Design Dreams

Rather than stories or plays, some dreams focus on designs or arrangements of shapes and forms They may be dreams which feature structural details, such as workers constructing a foundation or building according to a certain geometric plan, or a special pattern, such as the accenting paint trim around the windows of a house or a very distinctive pattern for a dress. In these cases, it is often possible to draw the design or arrangement. What seems important to the dreamer may be something about the design or about the relationship between the forms.

A man in a mid-life identity search had a dream of an historic building on the main street of the town where he had lived as a boy. It was an early Methodist meeting house which had been restored. As he toured the building, he was fascinated by its unique design: it was square and each of the three storeys was turned at a 45–degree angle to the one below so that there were many bevelled angles which allowed for windows looking in many different directions. It also permitted stairs going up and down to pass each other easily. The dream seemed to be relating something important about the structure of his Methodist heritage. The design of the building had a very centering feel to it and suggested a diamond with its many facets.

In another dream, the same man was given a large turtle (often a symbol of totality, of the foundation of the world) to hold. The instructions were not clear, but he got the idea that he was to see how he could keep it under control without hurting it. He held it with his fingers by the sides of the shell, but the turtle was frightened and squirmed with its legs trying to brush his fingers away. The man then tried to devise a cage to hold it. He made some wire rectangles that were hinged like the pages of a book; but

with the "book" of frames only partway open, as he had
them, he realized they would only half cover the turtle
and the hinge pin would go right through where the
middle of the turtle would be. The man who gave him the
turtle came and asked how he was doing. Then that man
rearranged the wire frames so they were splayed out
enough to cover the whole turtle. "I knew that somehow I
had to make the central hinge go only so deep," he said,
"so the turtle could exist beneath it. The man in my dream
altered it miraculously." Here the geometric problem of
fitting the large turtle into a cage of limited frames
became the central symbol of the dream.

Dreaming—A Personal Experience

The above list of dream experiences is by no means
exhaustive. Each dreamer has her own unique form and
style of dreaming. I have outlined these particular aspects
of dream experience to whet the reader's own appetite.
By describing others' dreams, I hope to help focus the
reader's own dream experience and to zero in on
dreaming as a regular experience of our life. Dreams and
dream interpretations belong to a strange foreign world
until it is your dream and it shouts your name.

In working toward a method of interpreting dreams,
therefore, I want to begin with the experience of
dreaming itself. It would be helpful if you, the reader,
were to pause for a moment and reflect on what you
experience when you dream. At this point we are not
looking at the actual content of the dream, only at what
the experience of dreaming is like for you. What kind of a
world does it put you into? How is that world different
from your waking experience? How real is the
experience? What form do your dreams usually take? that
of a story or play? that of a design or configuration? or

something else? What does it usually feel like to have had a dream?

Those who don't remember their dreams or believe that they don't dream might experiment using some of the techniques for dream recall outlined in chapter 6. Often I have found that with encouragement, a sense of expectancy and a welcoming attitude, dreams may come to those who previously did not remember having any.

The Intrigue of Dreams

Currently, there is a surging interest in dreams which I believe goes beyond mere curiosity or amusement. It reflects a widespread fascination with the unconscious, a deep longing to touch the mystery of what lies hidden within the soul. This is part of the modern desire to understand ourselves better. The inner world has become the new frontier. For some, it is also part of the quest to find the springs of creativity and to unlock energy and potentiality. In addition, there is a hunger for spiritual reality, to be in touch with that which gives life meaning. For many modern people, traditional values no longer hold. They are suspicious of a merely dogmatic religion and bored with formal ritual, which they see as empty. In the current religious vacuum, many people are seeking for personal experience that will transform and fulfil life. So today's strong interest in dreams may be seen as meeting the almost religious need for experience which will help guide one's daily life and put a person in touch with her personal truth.

What excited me most when I first began to listen to my dreams was this sense that I was in touch with a great mystery. Something powerful seemed to be at work in my dreams, something that possessed a wisdom and purpose beyond my conscious mind. It was as if there were someone who knew me better than I knew myself who was directing the dreams which came to me. That "someone" seemed to have an intimate knowledge of the important factors in my conscious life at the time, would offer a point of view, or grapple with some aspect of a life issue, or indicate a direction to go. A good example is a dream I had in 1978 when I was struggling with the decision whether to leave the pastoral ministry to do doctoral studies in psychotherapy in Boston. Part of the dream is as follows:

My family and I are travelling in the United States and on the way back, at a city in Vermont, are involved in a celebration— an historical pageant that reenacts a battle in the War of 1812 (although I feel it is the Seven Years' War between England and France). At one point I am in the turretted castle-like building looking down on the battle competition. Squads of uniformed young men are competing to see who can win by holding a strategic position. They are beautifully dressed in period uniforms, ruffles, tricorner hats, leggings and frock coats, much like the French and English of the seventeenth and eighteenth centuries. I am looking down from the third or fourth floor of the castle. It seems like a fairyland of trees, hills and valleys, and several squads of soldiers are fighting below in the pathways and courtyards. One group is declared the winner: they have captured a position and are holding it.

The scene shifts. I am on the ground floor in the doorway of the main building. A protective older woman is with me and a captain of the guard of the groups that have been fighting. I, too, am in uniform and am one of them. The officer is reporting to the woman and me that, although they have tried to keep me from leaving, they aren't able to. The battle has been fought and the decision made. Reluctantly, he is reporting that I will be leaving. He salutes as if I am his superior, wishes me well and departs.

The scene shifts to the shores of a mountain lake. A church conference is being held at a resort. Again, I am leaving. A woman rebukes me for the way I conducted a portion of the conference, saying that I didn't try hard enough to get passage of some people to the conference. Boats could have been sent for them, but weren't. I listen to the condemnation and remain silent and wait out her anger. In my heart, I know I did all I could.

At the time of the dream, I was deeply divided in trying to make the decision. The dream portrays that a battle, or rather the reenactment of a battle, has gone on, and identifies the battle with a decision, which has been made, for me to leave. What it said to me was that the decision to go had already been made and had been accepted, but with great internal reluctance and hostility. There are elements of the dream which I won't go into, such as the French-English association and the War of 1812, which likely have some connection to my English and French ancestry and my United Empire Loyalist forebears who left the United States through Vermont following the American War of Independence. I was impressed, both with the ancestral scope of the dream and with the imaginative way the dream expressed the current struggle that I was in, and how it crystallized for me where my feelings really stood. The image of the officer reporting the decision and honoring me with his salute gave me courage to pursue my goal and to withstand the fierce anger of that part of me that would have held me to the church. This illustrates how images of violence and fighting in dreams, with or without guns, often identify issues of conflict and anger, in this case, I believe, on an internal level. I say "internal" in this case, rather than being some external source of anger, for several reasons: because, with the exception of the reference to "my family," the rest of the dream is peopled by anonymous figures, because of the uniform which I, the dreamer, wear in common with the soldiers, the further fact that the anonymous people reported to me as the central authority, and because of the relevance of the church setting to my vocational struggle.

One of my reasons for writing this book is to share my excitement about dreams. This common, almost universal, experience of humanity offers a source of insight and help for living, if we can find a way of understanding dreams. My purpose in this book is to lay out a method of working with one's own dreams that does not require special knowledge of symbols or of psychological processes. To be sure, that kind of special expertise is necessary for in-depth analysis of dreams, and, in cases of emotional or mental disturbance, the guidance of a trained analyst is required. But most normal people, who are able to cope realistically with everyday life, can gain fresh insight into themselves through a laymen's approach to dream interpretation.

Some dreams have fairly obvious meanings and you may gain benefit simply by taking time to reflect on them yourself. More complex dreams can be opened to levels of understanding through application of the method that will be outlined here. Working either alone or with a close friend, you should be able to apply the step-by-step format I will outline. There are no guarantees, however, only opportunities for learning and experimenting to unravel the secrets of our dreams.

Before we describe the actual format of dream analysis, it is important that we realize what is involved in this unique phenomenon of dreams. What physical processes are involved in dreaming? Where do dreams come from? Do dreams have meaning? What is the role and power of symbols in dreams? Many people are skeptical about finding meaning in their dreams. They may doubt that there is anything more to dreams than a natural discharge of mental energy during sleep. When anyone suggests that dreams may come from an unknown realm of wisdom, either divine or from the human unconscious, they raise their eyebrows. It would be helpful, therefore, to explore this phenomenon and consider what may be involved in dreams. We may find that dreams have far more credibility than we had previously thought.

2
WHAT IS DREAMING?

The mystery of dreams has intrigued humans in all ages, inspiring some, haunting others, baffling all. There are many ways in which humans have tried to make sense of dreams. In *The Book of Lambspring*, written in 1625, Nicholas Barnaud Delphinas wrote a highly poetic view of dreams:

> Be warned and understand truly
> That two fishes are swimming in our sea,
> The vastness of which no man can describe.
> Moreover the Sages say
> That the two fishes are only one, not two;
> They are two, and nevertheless they are one.

A sense of the mystery of dreams was caught by Sidney Lanier in his "Hymns of the Marshes," written in 1870:

> And now from the Vast of the Lord will the waters of
>   sleep
> Roll in on the souls of men,
> But who will reveal to our waking ken
> The forms that swim and the shapes that creep
>   Under the waters of sleep?
> And I would that I could know what swimmeth below
>   when the tide comes in
> On the length and the breadth of the marvellous
>   marshes of Glynn.

Many ancient Greeks believed that, when we dream, the soul leaves the body and goes to the world of the gods. Other Greeks, such as Aristotle, thought that dreams were a natural mental process in which the soul randomly reexperiences the day's events, a view which has become very influential in shaping the modern attitude and is widely held in the Muslim world. On the other hand, some in the ancient world regarded dreaming as "lunacy," a nighttime insanity when humans came under the spell of the moon, which in Latin is "luna."

Scientific Studies of Dreaming

Until recently, the process of dreaming was not directly accessible to scientific study. No one knew exactly how to tell whether another person was dreaming. Investigators only had the report of the dreamer as to the contents of the dream or whether the person had dreamed at all. We still do not know exactly how much correspondence there is between the dream as reported and the dream as dreamed.

The correlation of dreaming with eye movement was made as early as 1892 by G. T. Ladd. In 1938, Jacobson corroborated Ladd's suspicions by observing that the eyes actually do move during dreaming. The first scientific study of objective factors relating to dreaming was reported in 1953 by Aserinsky and Kleitman who, during a study of eye movement in adults, observed bursts of rapid eye movements (REM's) during sleep. Using electroencephelogram (EEG) leads from two skin spots adjacent to the eye and by monoriting heart and respiratory rates, they observed that "jerky rapid eye movements," taking only a fraction of a second, occurred in clusters for 5 to 60 minutes during sleep. These REM's were associated with a low voltage EEG pattern and significantly higher heart and respiratory rates.

William C. Dement, another researcher associated with Kleitman, went further to establish the connection between what he called "REM sleep" and dreaming. He found that subjects who were awakened during REM sleep reported being in the midst of dreaming, whereas those who were awakened out of non-REM sleep seldom reported being in a dream. He also discovered that the amount of REM sleep allowed before a subject was awakened corresponded to the length of their dream reports. The work of Dement and Kleitman led to the establishment of a standard way of identifying stages of sleep. This involved combined measurement of brain waves, eye movements and muscle tension. Now there was a way to gather external evidence associated with dream activity and to answer such puzzling questions as how often and how long we dream, whether some people don't dream or whether all people dream, but some do not remember their dreams.

The Four Stages of Sleep

From the extensive sleep studies which followed, we have learned that there are four stages of sleep. Here I rely on the summary given by Stephen LaBerge in his excellent book *Lucid Dreaming*.[1] From a waking state, you experience drowsiness as you enter Stage 1, which is very light sleep. There is a change in the alpha rhythm of brain waves, and slow eye movements and decreased muscle tone are evident. Normally, this stage only lasts a few minutes as you descend into a deeper Stage 2 sleep. Here there are slow waves and high frequency "spindles" showing on the EEG. There is little eye movement and further decreased muscle tone. If you are a light sleeper, you might report lengthy and vivid dreams during this stage. Movement into Stage 3 follows, with the increase of high-amplitude slow waves, which culminates in Stage 4 when these "delta" waves dominate the EEG. This is the deepest stage of sleep and in this state there are no eye movements and muscle tone is low. All of this normally takes place in the first ninety minutes of sleep. Then the process is reversed and you move back through Stage 3 and Stage 2 to Stage 1. But this time, as you return to Stage 1, your muscle tone has reached its lowest possible level and there is a dramatic increase in rapid eye movements. This is called "ascending Stage 1 REM" or "active sleep" and eighty to ninety percent of those awakened from it report vivid, often detailed, dreams.

Typically, you go through three or four such cycles each night, thus having three or four vivid dreaming times. As the cycle unfolds, an important progression takes place in the length and frequency of the REM periods. The REM period, which in its first occurrence usually lasts from five to fifteen minutes, becomes longer with each cycle, extending to forty minutes, even an hour or more, late in the sleep cycle. Also, while the REM periods are lengthening, the interval between them decreases in length. This means that the percentage of dream time increases the longer you sleep. LaBerge estimates that in seven hours of sleep half of your dreaming time comes in the last two hours and that, if you could sleep an extra hour, it would be almost all dreaming time. So, if you want to increase your dream activity, sleep longer.

How long does it take to dream a dream? Is it instantaneous, as in the traditional story of Mohammad's Night Journey? In this story the Prophet overturned a pitcher of water just as he was leaving to make a tour of the seven heavens, via flying horse. He met with seven prophets, numerous angels and God himself before he returned to his bed, only to find that the water had not yet run out of the pitcher. Sometimes a dream can be so compact and "out of time" as to seem briefer than a moment. However, sleep studies show that dreams do not happen in an instant, as we sometimes suppose. Normally, it takes about the same time as the action would take in real life.

REM and other studies show that everyone dreams every night whether they recall the dreams or not. Certain abnormal states, however, such as high fever, and the use of alcohol and some drugs, may interrupt or distort dreaming.

There is evidence that dreaming fulfils a necessary mental health function. Those who were awakened at the beginning of REM sleep or prevented from REM sleep for several nights were found to exhibit behavior bordering on illness. Dreaming appears to function, in part, as a way of mentally assimilating the meaning of the day's events and digesting it into an integrated process.

Some studies show that external factors such as changes in temperature, air pressure and sounds have little influence on the dream. However, powerful images or complex forms of stimulation, such as movies shown before a person retires, apparently influence some dreams.

Dreams as Perception: Dreams as Imagination

One of the big questions that comes out of the many studies of dreaming over the past forty years is whether dreams depend upon what we have perceived in our waking environment or upon a more abstract symbol-making process of the brain. Are dreams a reworking of what we have actually seen and sensed or do they depend upon imagery and are thus works of imagination?

In an excellent recent book, Harry Hunt[2] summarizes the debate between these two positions. Those who think dreams are based on perception say that imagery itself depends on previous perception and does not require a particular symbolic ability. They point to the way in which our dreams are expressed in much the same terms as our waking experience of the world. In dreams, our central nervous system is activated in a way that closely reproduces the features of its waking functioning; and the "scanning" eye movements involved in REM sleep seem to be reviewing what was seen in waking life. Also supporting the notion that dreams are perceptual processes is a striking study in which subjects wore red-tinted goggles when awake. They reported having dreams in which red figured more prominently than all other colors. This red effect was especially strong in the earliest REM periods of sleep suggesting that perception plays a greater role in dreams in the onset of REM sleep and less in the later, more thought-like, non-REM dreams.

In contrast, those who think dreaming is a form of imagination say that dreaming is based on what we "know" rather than what we "see." They argue that it is impossible for dreaming to be a kind of perception because our eyes are closed in sleep. They find support for their position, that dreaming is a symbolic process of imaging, in studies of the dreams of those whose perception was restricted and who therefore could only be dreaming on some other basis than what they had seen: partially blind subjects had visually precise dreams of environments they had never actually seen, but only as they imagined them to be; and women with Turner's syndrome, an hereditary condition that limited their spatial perception, had dreams of imageless thought that was simply "known," and with no perceived detail whatever.

It is difficult to come down clearly on one side or the

other in this debate, for, as Hunt finds, there is equal support for both positions and some research, such as that on the dreams of recent amputees with phantom limbs, shows that some subjects dream as they "sense" and some as they "know." Moreover, the early experiments showing a close correspondence between REM-state eye movement patterns and the movement in dream events have been difficult to replicate. While the many studies of dreaming that have been done are fascinating, they have not been conclusive about the nature of dreaming.

The anticipation that studying REM sleep would greatly open our understanding of dreams has not been fulfilled. The association of dreaming with REM sleep is no longer certain. Although REM sleep most often coincided with dreaming, as reported by the subject, it is evident that some dreaming takes place during non-REM sleep in the sleep cycle. We know that some people dream even during catnaps of ten minutes or less. Dreaming also can take place under hypnosis, during daydreams, or in other waking states, using guided fantasy, for example. There is obviously more involved in dreaming than is explained by our current understanding of sleep cycles and REM sleep.

The difficulty in proving a scientific connection between dreaming and REM sleep has led some researchers to ask whether the two are related at all. Some have argued that dreaming may be one outcome of certain brain activity that may frequently also cause REM activity.

The fact that dreams are a completely private experience and beyond verification leads some skeptics to question the reality of dreams themselves. To them, dreams are illusions. Describing the difficulty of taking dreams seriously from a biological standpoint, one researcher says: "All we have is the uncertain memory of some visions, thoughts or feelings that lingered from sleep. Skeptics would argue that the reality of dreaming is an inference based on circumstantial evidence."[3] Others scoff that the only meaning the word "dream" has is in reference to the strange tales we report to each other, not to anything that can be proven to have occurred.

Yet the overwhelming evidence of dreams remains. Almost universally, human beings report this experience in one form or another. That it is personal and private, and ultimately subjective, creates problems for the kind of science that demands objective verification; but we must not let that discredit it as personal experience. In the science of human being, we are what we study. Try as we will, we cannot stand outside ourselves or measure our own experience objectively. Perhaps the most essential parts of ourselves can only be known subjectively. Viewed in this way, the fact that dreams are so private and hidden could indicate that they belong to that most central and unique aspect of ourselves.

Rather than dismiss dream experience as "illusion" or "inference" because it does not fit our measuring instru-ments, we need to recognize that dreams are necessarily private and nonetheless real or valuable for that. It is an essential feature of dreams and not to be lamented. As Harry Hunt asks, "Can we even begin to study the dream without acknowledging it first and foremost as an immediately experienced subjective state?" The point of view taken in this book is that dream experience validates itself. The more important question is what are we to make of this puzzling, enthralling phenomenon?

3
WHERE DO DREAMS COME FROM?

The outstanding work done in sleep studies over the last forty years has advanced our understanding of dreaming as a complex mental activity. But dreams themselves are more than the mental process of dreaming. To describe them simply in terms of brain waves only partly explains their nature and origin. Just as an artist's painting is infinitely more than paint being applied to canvas, so a dream is more than the impulses of the brain which transmits it.

In his book *Alternate Realities*, Lawrence Le Shan makes a similar point with regard to music by asking us to imagine a pianist sitting down at a piano and pressing the keys with his fingers. Notes of music vibrate in the air and presently we are aware of enjoying the melody. But where did the melody come from? It is not the specific notes being played; because the pianist could play in an entirely different key, striking a different range of notes, and yet we would still hear the same melody. Where did the melody come from? "It seems clear," says LeShan, "that for the melody to exist our contribution is needed. We are part of its creation.... It is only there if someone listens to the notes, and contributes to its coming into existence."[4] In a similar way, a dream presents us with mental pictures which in themselves may be meaningless. A receptive dreamer is required who will listen to the dream in such a way that the theme or melody becomes clear. This is the

28

role of interpretation. The dreamer makes connections between the images of the dream and the events of his daily life, and thus finds a message in the dream. In Le Shan's sense, we contribute to its creation by realizing the significance of the dream images.

But even before we realize the theme of a dream, or recognize the "melody," so to speak, the theme is already there, waiting to be discovered. As if there were a mind at work behind the dream which is responsible for its production. Most people have this sense of some connecting idea or purpose which lies behind the story, or series of dream images. Dreams are amazing mental and emotional achievements, employing a high order of organization and creativity. In waking life we would be hard-pressed to conjure up the intricate stories and amazing images that dreams spin out nightly.

When we dream we experience something that surprises us with its originality. Dreams, for the most part, come unbidden, with a mind of their own. They possess a wisdom and knowledge that often amazes us. Morton Kelsey, who has written widely about dreams, tells of an unusual experience he had before he first published any of his writing.[5] A man dreamed the name of a publisher who was interested in Kelsey's work before Kelsey himself had the information. This same man later brought him a dream about the contents of a letter which no one, other than Kelsey and the writer, who lived at some distance, had read. It was this kind of amazing knowledge that so impressed me when I first began to pay attention to my dreams. They possessed not only a detailed personal knowledge of my life but also a wisdom beyond my conscious understanding, as if someone with access to a broad vision of my life, past, present and future, were nudging me toward what would benefit my growth and development.

It is this truth of the "other" in dreams, who speaks so knowingly of our life situation, that makes dreams such an adventure. Something important is to be learned, vast resources of personal wisdom are to be tapped, all of which may be beyond, even quite contrary to, our conscious understanding at the moment. In Jung's words: "In each of us there is another whom we do not know. He speaks to us in dreams and tells us how differently he sees us from the way we see ourselves." So there seems to be something powerful and purposeful working behind our dreams—a mysterious "other"—yet this hidden source of dreams is very much connected to us, indeed, seems to be a part of ourselves. What could this be?

Many in the ancient and modern worlds have believed that dreams come from God. The ancient Greeks believed, as I mentioned earlier, that, when a person dreamed, the soul left the body and visited with the gods. Most religions have the sense that dreams are a source of revelation. Dreams give the kind of insights, wisdom and direction which can be called religious. Through dreams, the reality of a spiritual, non-physical world encounters us. We may say that dreams offer evidence of a direct connection with the divine, the sacred realm of God.

In my own life the discovery of dreams as a source of revelation brought a new dimension of vitality to my religious life. There was an immediacy and personal quality to God's presence in my daily affairs when each night dreams tracked and commented on the day's events and thoughts. There is a sense of guidance for daily living that comes through dreams.

Many modern people, however, would prefer to think of dreams psychologically, rather than religiously. In our time, the ancient wisdom of the dream has been linked with the unconscious. Carl Jung (1875-1961), the renowned Swiss psychoanalyst who pioneered in the interpretation of dreams, recognized the shift from a religious to a psychological understanding of dreams:

> For modern man it is hardly conceivable that a God existing outside ourselves should cause us to dream, or that the dream foretells the future prophetically. But if we translate this into the language of psychology, the ancient idea becomes much more comprehensible. The dream, we could say, originates in an unknown part of the psyche and prepares the dreamer for the events of the following day.[6]

That "unknown part of the psyche" we call the unconscious. The word "psyche" refers to the whole of human personality, both conscious and unconscious. We may think of dreams, then, as coming from a world of wisdom and knowledge within us which, because it is hidden from consciousness, may be called the unconscious. If someone is unconscious, we think that person is unknowing or unaware. Not so with the unconscious part of ourself. We call it "unconscious" not because it is unknowing or unaware but because we are not conscious of it. Judging from the intimate knowledge of ourselves in our dreams, it is well aware of us. Far from being asleep, this part is aware not only of everything we think and do and experience, but knows everything that happens to us, both outside and inside. Bringing its wisdom into our conscious life is important for our growth and development as mature people.

To speak of dreams as coming from the unconscious raises a basic question. If the source of dreams is hidden from consciousness, how can we know anything about it?

This might also be said of other things we cannot see directly, such as electricity or gravity or the wind. Because they are not directly seen or "knowable," they can only be studied by inference, and described in terms of the effects they produce. This is especially so of the unconscious.

Hypnosis

One major evidence of the reality of the unconscious is offered by hypnosis. Sigmund Freud was one of the first to use hypnosis to reveal the unconscious mind. He encountered several patients suffering from anxiety whose cases resisted all treatment until they were put under hypnosis; then the symptoms disappeared. Through hypnosis the crucial material which had been hidden from consciousness, because it was offensive, came to awareness.

Similar results are seen in warfare when an occasional soldier in front line action would become paralyzed in the trigger hand or arm. When sent back for treatment, often it was found that these loyal soldiers were pacifist and their moral conflict with patriotism was resolved by the unconscious paralyzing them so they could not offend their pacifism.

The immense power of the unconscious may also be seen in any stage hypnotist's demonstration of making a subject's body go totally rigid, for example, and able to bear considerable weight when stretched between two chairs, simply by the power of suggestion.

Physiological Evidence

The unconscious also shows itself in those automatic responses that our bodies make to certain situations. There are parts of our brain that are susceptible to suggestion. Some people, for example, are able, with suggestion, to raise the temperature in one part of their body and cool another part. There are also unconscious body responses such as tics and rashes which express hidden meanings. By calling these "psychosomatic" symptoms, we are recognizing the influence of the unconscious mind on the body. The unconscious is as real as blushing.

Association Experiment

The reality of the unconscious was also demonstrated by Jung's Association Experiment in which he asked a person to say the first word that came into his mind after certain words were said and the response time was measured. Unusual delays or bizarre associations were deemed to indicate areas of unconscious resistance reflecting troubled experiences long since "forgotten" by consciousness but remembered by the all-knowing unconscious.

Habit

From these brief inferences, we come to see how powerful and immense the unconscious is. It is commonly said that we are only using a small fraction of our brain, that consciousness is just the tip of the iceberg, and beneath lie vast resources. We have only touched part of our potential. Actually, the unconscious plays a much more active part in our daily life than we commonly recognize. Driving a car, for example, is largely an unconscious function. That is not so when we are in the beginning stages, when every turn is deliberately made, and we are in a constant state of alert. But once the basics are mastered and become habitual we relax into a smooth automatic performance that is mostly unconscious. Adding the use of a carphone while driving shows even more how complex tasks, once learned, rely heavily on the unconscious. The same principle applies to many other habitual practices as well, such as dancing, typing or playing golf.

Put in this wider context, dreams are just one example of the unconscious at work. Freud said that dreams were the "royal road to the unconscious," that is, the best way of entering into a territory which is cloaked in mystery.

The idea of the unconscious has been developing over the last two hundred years and in the twentieth century has become one of the greatest areas of scientific discovery. Early in the century, Jung became one of the foremost pioneers in exploring the unconscious. Finding close parallels between physics and psychology, he believed that the unconscious was a source of tremendous potential, that the unlocking of the mysteries of the psyche would release energy as great as that released by the splitting of the atom. Limitless resources of wisdom which had been hidden in mystery, untapped and un- available, would become known and available to guide human thought and action.

This was a somewhat different view than Freud's in which the unconscious was thought to be like a closed container holding thoughts and memories that were not welcome in one's conscious mind. Freud regarded the unconscious as a place beneath consciousness, like a cellar, where material that was too shameful or offensive for conscious recognition, could be stored and forgotten. In contrast, Jung found the unconscious to be open to unlimited depths, and not just restricted to the individual's own life but joining her to material that was held in common with the whole of humanity. It contained a kind of human racial heritage as well as contents unique to each individual.

A powerful factor in convincing Jung of the great depth of the unconscious and of its underlying oneness with all of humanity was a dream he had which showed the personal and collective unconscious as levels below levels in the cellar of his house. In the dream, Jung was on the first floor in his house. The room was nicely furnished in eighteenth-century style. Seeing a staircase, he decided to descend to the ground floor where he noticed the structure and heavy old furniture to be of the sixteenth century or earlier. Thinking there might be a cellar, he went down a dusty, worn staircase and found a very old setting with Roman bricks and a flagstone floor. Holding a lantern in his hand, he thought he was surely at the bottom. But then in a corner he noticed a square stone with a ring in it. He lifted this and found himself peering down into a lower cellar which was very dark, like a cave. As light filtered down he saw that it was filled with prehistoric pottery, bones and skulls. He felt he had made an important discovery.[7]

Jung's Model of the Psyche

In the model of the psyche which Jung held, consciousness would be like a shallow layer sitting above an unknown depth of unconsciousness, much like the tip of the iceberg. Beneath it lie unfathomed depths of mystery. If we think of individuals' consciousness as islands in the ocean (A, B, and C in Fig. 1), then the unconscious would be like the underwater foundation that goes down to bedrock. That underwater foundation would correspond to what Jung calls the "personal unconscious" which contains contents which are unique to each individual, A, B and C. This part of the unconscious. contains those repressed items of which Freud spoke, as well as material belonging to the specific individual which has not yet come into consciousness. This is all personal unconscious.

Beneath the personal unconscious lies the "collective unconscious." In Figure 1, the bedrock on which the foundation of each island stands and which joins islands below the surface corresponds to this "collective unconscious." It contains images that are common to humanity, shown here as A, B and C. He found that certain images are universal; for example, that aborigines in Africa and Australia dream in the same basic symbols as stockbrokers in New York City. His reason for believing in a collective unconscious stemmed from these common elements, from the dream he had had, and from the observation that some dreams have significance beyond the individual who dreamed them.

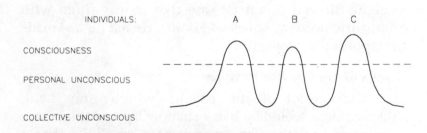

FIGURE 1

Some dreams appear to have access to knowledge of other peoples' lives and this clairvoyance may be explained by the psychological connection that could exist through the deep unconscious. The following is an example of this telepathic quality of dreams. A woman, who was in an abusive marriage, saw in her dream the face of a former boyfriend, whom she had not seen for many years. He kept saying to her, "I need you." The dream recurred several times and each time she brushed it aside, until a very powerful dream came in which her mother appeared and said emphatically, "Will you please call him?" When she awoke, she hardly knew where to begin but finally reached him by phone. The dream had given her courage to act. He was surprised and glad to hear from her. He told her he was going through the most difficult time in his whole life and had thought of her almost daily although they had been out of touch for over fifteen years. The phone call and their reconnection ultimately led to the woman leaving her abusive husband and marrying her former boyfriend. This illustrates how dreams can have a telepathic aspect, connecting us at a deep level, in spite of physical distance.

This ability to make immediate connection with the unconscious gives dreams part of their special power. While there are many ways in which the unconscious speaks—art, religion, music and dance, folklore and fairytales, intuitions, "coincidences," personal insights and discoveries—dreams are among the foremost. Dreams provide unique access to the unconscious.

Dreams represent in symbolic form what the unconscious is saying to the person's consciousness, whose center we call the "ego." They are like a bridge between the unconscious and conscious minds over which new material may come into conscious awareness. What the conscious part of us, the ego, remembers, receives and acts upon, by integrating it into conscious life, becomes the pattern for our journey to wholeness. Only what is caught, received and integrated by consciousness benefits ego growth: what is forgotten, denied or unused is lost.

The sewing machine offers an everyday image of this process. In an ordinary sewing machine, there are two threads, an upper thread, which is threaded through the needle, and a lower thread, held on a bobbin beneath the material being sewn (Fig. 2). The descending needle, with upper thread attached, hooks the lower thread pulling it to the surface where it is caught before the needle goes down to draw another stitch up. These stitches that are caught and held on the surface become the pattern.

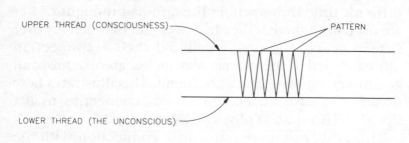

FIGURE 2

In a similar way, when dreams are remembered, images which were previously unconscious are caught by consciousness and become part of a meaningful pattern that integrates both conscious and unconscious inputs. Consciousness is thereby enlarged and transformed in the direction of personal growth and development. When dream-symbols are accepted and assimilated into consciousness, they transform the ego in its self-understanding. A new energy is added. A new or enlarged attitude is evident.

With this understanding of the unconscious, dreams take on a special significance. They connect a person not only with the hidden or unconscious depths of himself, but also make available the resources of a world-psyche and the wisdom of ages of human living, what Jung called "racial history." So dreams can be a source of identity and guidance far beyond the limited scope of one's own personality. It is not merely a matter of what meaning dreams might have, but how dreams might empower and transform human consciousness with the energy of that collective mind. Here psychology and religion overlap. The word "psyche" refers to "soul." What humans are doing when they dream is getting in touch with their souls. Thus, by putting us in touch with our unconscious, dreams are fulfilling the role which the ancient Greeks saw in dreams, that of connecting us with the divine, whether that is seen as external or as power coming from within each individual.

4
DO DREAMS HAVE MEANING?

Almost everyone wants to know what his dream might mean. When the teller in the bank learned that I was writing a book about dreams, she immediately volunteered that earlier that day a customer had told her he'd had a dream in which he saw his father lying in a coffin. "In real life he's not dead," the man had said. "In fact he's going to fly tomorrow. Should I warn him not to go?" Hardly had she finished telling me this than another teller came over and asked me, "What does a flood of muddy water mean? In my dream last night my husband and I were trying to hold back a flood of water that was threatening to get into our basement." Such is the fascination and intrigue of dreams.

Personal Meaning

Dreams, by the very way they present themselves, suggest that they have an importance. They grab our attention, at one extreme, by the fantastic or mysterious quality they often embody and, at the other extreme, by referring frequently to realistic aspects of our lives with which we are undeniably familiar. Offering a new view of some known person or situation in our lives, as some dreams do, suggests a possible message for our consideration, while the more imaginative kind of dream offers to transform our mundane experience. Also, the fact that some dreams tell a story, are intense or disturbing, implies that a meaning may lie within them.

40

For these and other reasons, it is inviting to think that dreams have a meaning for our personal lives and that they offer a larger view than we already have. Any phenomenon as widespread and engaging as dreams must have some significance.

Difficulty Finding a Single Sure Meaning

But serious problems lie in the path of being sure of such meanings. Dreams are often vague and jumbled. Some dream images are indistinct or fragmentary. Can we be sure we have recalled all the important parts of a dream? The most significant clue may lie in a part of a dream we have forgotten. Some dreams seem to defy all interpretation. Many dreams are open to multiple interpretations. How can we be sure which interpretation is correct or that dreams have any meaning that could be valid for our lives? There are really two questions involved here: Do dreams have meaning? And if so, what kind of meaning do dreams have?

Do Dreams Have Meaning?

Some say that dreams are meaningless. Foulkes, for example, an authority on dream research, writes: "The reason why dreamers can't understand what their dreams mean, and why we have such difficulty constructing adequate accounts of what they might have meant, is that they didn't mean anything."[8] Dreams are deemed just a random mental activity, or a neurological blip, as irrelevant to the meaning of our life as an itch. Those who hold this position speak of dreams as "froth" (Robert) or as a "neural dumping" (Crick and Mittison) of material left over from the day. They regard dreams as a spin-off of recent experiences, a clearing of memory. Others see dreams as an afterglow of the day's events, a regurgitation of the nightly TV news, for example, or a response to something we ate.

Others would limit the possible meaning of dreams, for example, excluding dreams of paralysis, falling, flying or sexual arousal from having any personal significance because they regard these to be purely the products of physical bodily processes (Hobson and McCarley) and thus impersonal.

For some it is not merely a matter of the meaning of dreams; they question the very reality of dreams itself. Because dreams cannot be shown to another person and proven to have actually happened, dreams are dismissed by some as "illusions" or "an inference based entirely on circumstantial evidence," as we saw earlier in chapter 2. Shadowy memories recalled through the fogs of sleep do not provide much by way of a substantial basis for meaning. Some skeptics have argued that a dream only appears to have a meaning, because it employs the same images as everyday life and gives the appearance of something familiar, when, in fact, it is a nonsensical parody.

One response to the difficult question of whether dreams have meaning has been to separate the phenomenon of dreams from any actual meaning within the dream itself by suggesting that the meaning is something that is added later by interpretations that are made. By giving a dream a meaning, we are seen as completing something which the dream only began. So the meaning may not be in the dream itself, but in the processing of the dream into conscious life, either with another person or in an internal dialogue with one's waking self. This might explain why meaning seems to flow better when you talk out your dream with another person. There can be an almost "electric" energy when people work together on one person's dream. It might also explain why the "obvious" meaning of a dream can sometimes elude the dreamer and occur more often to others with whom we share our dream than to oneself. Perhaps the "meaning" is an attempt to make sense consciously of something which in itself is neutral or ambiguous, just as we may try to give significance to coincidences that happen "out of the blue."

Dreams—a Source of Personal Meaning

On the other hand, there are those who have found very definite meaning in their dreams which came from the dream itself. There are, for example, cases of scientific discoveries which came precisely through dreams. A well-known instance is that of Friedrich Auguste Kekule von Stradonitz, the organic chemist, who first formulated the complex structure of the benzene molecule in the 1860's. He had labored unsuccessfully to learn the exact formulation of the benzene molecule. Then, he had a dream in which he saw before him a snake swallowing its tail. When he awoke, he realized that his dream had revealed to him, in precise detail, the helix structure of the molecule which had eluded him in his waking life. Albert Einstein similarly credited the power of the unconscious mind in sleep with providing the solution to some of the most difficult mathematical problems that challenged him.

Some celebrated authors have attributed some of their major creative works to the inspiration of dreams. Robert Louis Stevenson believed dreams to be the source of much of his best writing and specifically mentioned the development of Dr. Jekyll and Mr. Hyde in that connection. Samuel Taylor Coleridge, having fallen asleep while reading the exploits of Kubla Khan, the Mogul conqueror, reported that he awoke to write down the fully developed poem "Kubla Khan" which had been produced in his dream.

Dreams also have been the source of intimate knowledge about the dreamer's own medical condition. Carl Jung was once asked by a medical doctor to comment upon the dream of one of the physician's patients. The patient's dream was about lubricating machinery and there was also an image of a pond that had been drained to reveal the remains of two extinct animals, one a minute mastodon. Jung, with only the dream to go on, interpreted it to indicate the damming up of certain spinal fluid and was able to diagnose the man's condition as a particular form of epilepsy. The degree of accuracy involved in Jung's diagnosis astounded the man's doctor.[9]

There is no limit to the spheres in which dreams have added knowledge or skill to the personal waking life of individuals. Jack Nicklaus, the championship golfer, is said to have found a clue in his dreams which improved his golf score by ten strokes overnight! We might also cite cases in which people were given telepathic knowledge in dreams of events that happened simultaneously or in the future. All of this, then, supports the view that some dreams, at least, convey meaning that is appropriate, significant and beneficial to one's life and is far beyond coincidence.

Social Meaning

Sometimes dreams may pertain to a wider audience than the individual and have significance for that group. Some primitive tribes speak of "big dreams" which they believe have import for the whole tribe. Members of such tribes know that it is their duty to share such dreams with the whole tribe as a matter of common survival. Shortly before the First World War, Jung had such a dream in which a map of Europe was spread out before him. As he watched, a red flood rose and covered all of the countries on the map except the very highest mountainous areas, such as Switzerland. When he awoke, he knew that he had received a dream that was meant for the whole of humanity and was an ominous warning of the coming war. He sensed that this was a message which, at some level, all people had within them. It was one factor that added credence to his theory of the collective unconscious. Dreams which have telepathic messages or awarenesses partake of this same collective connection and should to be heeded and shared with others when appropriate.

Ancient Peoples

Another evidence that there is meaning in dreams comes from the widespread experience of ancient peoples that dreams were important sources of meaning. Ancient people knew and revered the power of dreams.

The Greeks and Romans accorded dreams an honored place in their societies. Although the ancient Greeks are remembered for their emphasis on reason and philosophy (which we might expect would be critical of dreams), they had a balanced philosophy which gave full recognition to the non-rational elements in human life. Accordingly, the most widely-held belief about dreams among the ancient Greeks was that dreams are a supernatural revelation, which they cherished. As mentioned earlier, they believed that during sleep the soul left the body and communed with the gods who entered "through the keyhole." In the visit, the god would be expressed to the sleeping person in a dream-figure or dream-image who was considered to be there in space, independent of the dreamer. So the Greeks didn't speak of having a dream, but of "seeing a dream."[10] There was, thus, an objectivity about the way they understood dreams to be given. The message was usually clear and the dreamer was expected to act upon it.

Besides these, what might be called objective dreams, the Greeks, in the time of Homer, also spoke of symbolic dreams, dreams that needed interpretation. Of course, these were more difficult to understand and out of that need there grew up whole schools of dream interpreters.

As one might expect, there were also minority views among the Greeks regarding dreams. As Morton Kelsey has detailed, about the fifth or sixth centuries B.C., a new idea gained popularity, similar to that held by early Hinduism and current today, that "the power of the dream comes from within the individual." He also mentions Aristotle's view that dreams are natural, not supernatural, and are likely to be "residual impressions left upon the soul by the previous day's activities." To relate dreams in this way to a natural human function was not to belittle the importance of dreams, however. Aristotle believed that dreams gave vital imformation: during sleep the soul was more aware of bodily sensations which, in themselves, could provide important messages to the dreamer. Generally, however, the ancient Greeks, and the Romans after them, regarded dreams as a valued communication from the sacred sphere to be received and heeded.

Biblical Traditions

The biblical traditions of both the Hebrew and Christian scriptures similarly regard dreams as revelation from God. When attention is paid to the richness and multiplicity of dreams in the Bible, it soon becomes obvious that there is an almost endless number—the dreams of Pharaoh and Joseph, Daniel and Nebuchadnezzar, Pilate's wife, Joseph and Peter—not to mention the vision and apocalyptic material in the books of Daniel and Revelation. It has been calculated that, if all of the dream and vision material in the Bible were gathered together, it would comprise approximately the same volume as the New Testament.

Yet, with the prevailing rationalism of the modern western world, this dream material has been almost totally ignored and repressed. The selective blindness of a culture to the spiritual springs of its birth and to the needs of its ongoing health is amazing. Only recently have we begun to recover from the reductionism of the age of reason that 250 years ago discredited the unconscious and dismissed its workings in dreams as superstition. So the resurgent interest in dreams in this century is really a rediscovery of an ancient wisdom. The belief that dreams have meaning is as old as humanity.

Primitive Peoples

That is not to say that belief in the meaning of dreams is a thing of the past. Primitive people living today have not forgotten the power and reality of dreams. Patricia Garfield[11] tells of the Senoi Indians of Malaysia who are known as the "dream people" because they treat dreams with great respect and use them in everyday life. Each morning they encourage the members of the family to tell their dreams and when children have dreams of monsters they teach them not to fear such things, but to give them a name and ask them what they want in their dreams. This particular tribe is noted for its mental health—no crime, no divorce, no violence, no mental illness. The Eskimo of Hudson Bay and the Patain Malay people are but two other native groups that take dreams with utmost seriousness. They believe that, during sleep, one's "soul" leaves the body to live in a special dream world. Further, it is considered dangerous to waken a sleeping person lest his "soul" would be lost, so real is the meaning of the dream journey.

To sum up, then, while some believe that dreams have no real meaning other than random brain activity, many others believe that dreams contain messages that apply to, and even have a vital influence on, their daily life. My experience is that dreams are meaningful and in this book I take the position that the meaning which flows from dreams can transform our lives.

Source of Meaning in the Unconscious

Once we say that dreams have a meaning beyond merely random mental energy, we are recognizing that there is another "mind" at work beyond what we know or think in our conscious mind. We may speak of that as our unconscious mind. Although dreams are expressed in terms and images that are usually familiar to our conscious mind, and often pertain to known situations, their roots are deep in the unknown reaches of the mind. The meaning of dreams comes from that hidden, mysterious reality, the unconscious.

We can go so far as to say that dreams have meaning only if we recognize the reality of the unconscious. "Without it," Jung said, "the dream is a mere freak of nature, a meaningless conglomeration of fragments left over from the day."[12] Only when we acknowledge that there is a dimension beyond what we know or experience consciously and that it has something to add to our knowledge and awareness, do dreams have any relevance. Otherwise there is no point looking to dreams for meaning; all that we would need to master life is deemed to be already present in our conscious mind and we can reason our way from there. What impressed me when I began to listen to dreams was that they reflected something real that lay beyond me and presented truths that I did not already possess consciously. To find a meaning in dreams, then, we must first accept the reality of the unconscious.

That may be more difficult than it sounds. When something is unseen and unknown, like the unconscious, it can be difficult to convince a person of its reality. It can also be a source of fear. In either case, it is not easy for many people to be willing to learn from such a hidden and mysterious source. Yet that is exactly what is required for a person to find the meaning of dreams. It is necessary to be humble and open toward what the ego does not know, in other words, to be open to the possibilities of being surprised.

There's a natural skepticism that has to be overcome. It is something that we encounter often at the beginning of analysis. The person hears that others, including the analyst, have found meaning in their dreams, but her own dreams have not had that sense for her. Most of us don't put much stock in the unconscious until we are given a dream that seizes us with some undeniable personal truth and convinces us. The businessman who had the dream of his fingers being half cut off, for example, "knew" that the warning about his work crowding out his creativity was real and had to be taken seriously. The task of dream interpretation involves learning what the unconscious is adding to our conscious knowledge or point of view, and then coming to terms with it.

Meaning in Context

The meaning of dreams comes out in the interplay between the images of the dream, given by the unconscious, and the life-situation to which the dream is addressed. However, it only comes through the creative connections made consciously by the dreamer who stands between the two. This is what Lawrence Le Shan meant in regard to music when he said we who hear the notes help create the melody. The meaning of a dream comes by opening up the various symbols or images of the dream through the dreamer's own associations, memories, intuitions. But it needs the circumstances of the dreamer's life and the connections to his experience to throw light on it. The context of the dreamer's life, whether it be some circumstance, question, problem or need, serves as a "hook" on which to hang the dream material, or as a "frame" to hold the dream picture.

In working with people's dreams and with my own, I have found it is a mistake to focus so much attention on the dream that the life-situation of the dreamer is neglected. Failure to be aware of the context of one's life-situation at the time of the dream can result in diminished meaning or in not finding a relevant "hook" to catch the dream's meaning at all. In terms of the sewing machine metaphor mentioned in chapter 3 (Fig. 2), consciousness, represented by the upper thread, includes consciousness of the context of one's life at the time of the dream. It is this, when combined with the input from the unconscious via a dream, that produces the meaningful pattern. Interpreting dreams, then, involves a twofold process of receiving the images given by the unconscious in dreams and then bringing them to the very real world of conscious daily experience. Later, in chapter 7, we will study certain techniques that help in this process.

What Kind of Meaning Do Dreams Have?

A more important question for many people than *whether* dreams have meaning is what *kind* of meaning they have. For them, it isn't that dreams lack meaning, but that it is difficult to be sure what the meaning is. How are we to interpret the material found in dreams? Which of several possible meanings will we choose? What do the various images represent? How do we know when the interpretation is true?

In a recent newspaper article, the writer spoke of how confusing dreams can be. There were so many possible meanings and different ways to interpret the various images in dreams, that she found it impossible to find a meaning she could depend upon. She said that for dreams to provide real "knowledge" the "message" would have to be certified as true. To illustrate her dilemma she referred to a dream of her husband's:

> He wanted to bet on the horses and a huge number flashed across the sky. It was long-distance, to Britain. He dialed the number to place his bet and a refined female voice responded; "This is Her Majesty, Queen Elizabeth II." They chatted, then he placed his bets.[13]

The writer's problem was how to know exactly what "Queen Elizabeth II" represents in the dream—Authority? England? Colonialism? Older women? or something else? She couldn't be sure of the "message" of the dream because she found the process of dream interpretation too variable and uncertain. Where was the authority to be found that could decide on the correct meaning?

Dream Meaning: Literal or Symbolic?

This is a familiar difficulty which is present in almost every dream. One of the main questions it raises is how literal or symbolic is the meaning in a dream?

Sorting Out the Kind of Meaning

To help decide whether a dream is to be taken literally or symbolically we may ask ourselves three basic questions.

(1) Who is the dream about? (objective and subjective meanings)

Is the dream about a person or a situation you know that is identified in the dream, or is the dream about you or an aspect of yourself? This is the question of whether the dream is primarily objective, about someone outside yourself, or primarily subjective, about yourself. That was the question raised by the man whose dream the bank teller relayed to me. In the man's dream, his father was in a coffin. In actual life, the father was alive and happened to be booked for a flight the next day. How could the man know whether his dream actually was a warning for his father not to take that flight? This is the problem of knowing how objective a dream is.

When we dream of someone we know, it is important to ask, does the dream actually pertain to that person's life or is it a projection of our own inner state? If the man's dream were taken *subjectively*, as pertaining to himself, several possibilities present themselves: it might mean that he had some anxiety about his father's well-being that attached itself to the fact of the coming flight; or the "father" in his dream might represent some aspect of himself, his feelings for his father, for example, or his relationship to his father; and the image of his father in a coffin might also indicate that, at some level within himself, he sees that relationship coming to an end. All of this might be conveyed by the dream quite apart from any risks of the airplane flight.

On the other hand, *objectively*, there are numerous instances of dreams in which a warning of disaster was foretold quite accurately. It may very well be that the dreamer was picking up some kind of telepathic message of an actual crash which was to befall his father. How can we know for sure?

Of course, we can't be sure. That kind of guaranteed certainty does not exist. Risk and faith are necessary conditions of human life. The best we can do is to consider fully the alternative meanings available and decide which one seems to apply best. Later, I will indicate a detailed method of sifting such meanings. For now, however, let us say that the basic principle to follow in making an interpretation is to go to the source. Inasmuch as the dream was not devised by his conscious mind and is a mystery to him, it is an expression of the depths within the psyche of the dreamer. Whatever prompted the dream lies within the dreamer and the most likely place to take up the traces of its meaning is within him. Which association or connection, therefore, seems to the dreamer to "fit"? Most often we will have what Eugene Gendlin calls a "felt sense" of the rightness of a meaning. It will "click" within the dreamer's awareness.

By "source," I also refer to the mystery which is greater than the individual dreamer and beyond his consciousness or intuition, what we might call "the giver of dreams," the divine Self, or God. Ultimately, if dreams have a personal meaning or direction for our lives, they embody a purpose that is pressing us in some direction. Getting in touch with that purpose, whether through prayer, meditation or just by being "open" and "expectant," is the ultimate foundation of valid dream interpretation.

In dreams where possible danger to another person or yourself is indicated, it is advisable to assume the worst. The man who dreamed of his father being dead might decide to tell his father the dream and of his concern for him. He could then let him decide whether to take the flight or not.

(2) What kind of message is it? (factual or metaphorical meanings)

Is the dream a statement of fact or is the dream to be taken figuratively? This may seem to be the same question as the previous one concerning objective or subjective meanings, but it is not. Here the question concerns not who the dream is about, whether in this case it applies to the father or to some aspect of the man doing the dreaming, but, rather, what is the nature of the message. Is the message a direct statement of fact or is the dream a metaphor? By metaphor, I mean an image that is used to represent something other than its literal role in the story.

Let me illustrate the difference between a factual and a metaphorical interpretation. If my dream of the battle between squads of eighteenth-century soldiers (pp. 16–17) were to be taken factually, it would mean that I understood it to be a replay of an actual experience I had and this would require me to believe I had had a past life in eighteenth-century Vermont. Considering the struggle I was going through making a decision at the time of the dream about going to study in Boston, I prefer to interpret the dream figuratively, taking the battle as a metaphor for my inner struggle, and the officer and angry woman to represent parts of my mental apparatus that had different attitudes toward my decision than I did. A further example of a factual meaning would be a dream in which the dreamer dreamed his house was on fire and awoke to find it so; or dreamed she had lost her job and awoke to remember that she had. In my experience, most dreams are of a metaphorical type.

(3) Is the meaning of the dream single-level or multi-level? (single or multiple meanings)

Is there more than one possible meaning from the dream? This was the difficulty of the woman whose husband had the betting dream involving Queen

Elizabeth. She wanted the dream to have a precise and certain meaning and was frustrated that dream symbols have various interpretations. "Queen Elizabeth" had to have a single, one-level meaning such as "authority" and nothing else. Anything less than that would not satisfy her requirement of what real "knowledge" or "objective truth" was.

Unfortunately, or fortunately, depending on your point of view, not all meaning is that simple or one-dimensional. Most meaning is symbolic, that is, there are many levels of meaning which may all be more or less true at the same time. "Queen Elizabeth" may represent England and colonialism and older women and authority all at the same time and could be tied in somehow with his choice of bet. Those who insist on the certainty of one-level meaning limit dreams to a factual level alone. This ignores the kinds of meaning that are subjective and private, such as the meaning of relationships and feelings. These are rich and varied and almost infinite in their shadings and complexities. Only layers of meaning could do justice to such feelings.

The dream of the man's father being in a coffin could be a dream in which the images were rich with multiple meanings. The dream could be reflecting the man's realization that his father is getting old and will not live forever. It could be expressing his anxiety about his father's mortality, or his feelings that the relationship with his father was in danger of ending, or that his father was not as important in his life as he used to be. It might even be a veiled wish that his father would die, possibly coming out of some deep, or hidden anger toward his father. In addition, it could be a warning that the plane might actually crash. It is possible that all of these, or a combination of them, could hold some truth for the dreamer. We can never say with certainty that a dream has only one limited meaning.

This means that no dream is ever completely interpreted. Symbols are liquid. Trying to pin the meaning of a symbol down simply to that given it by its place in a dream and in the surrounding context of the dreamer's life may attempt to make the symbol too definite and to fix it in a too-restricted meaning. Symbols defy such limitation. A symbol can be put into an infinite variety of settings and stories and its meanings poured out endlessly, never to be exhausted. Those who keep their dreams over time may have the experience of finding new vistas in old dreams. As they return to a dream they had worked with at some time in the past and thought they had plumbed its depths thoroughly, they may discover connections and depths of meaning they had never seen before. One reason may be that they themselves have grown in the interval, another may lie in the inexhaustible nature of symbols. It is this to which we turn in the next chapter.

Symbolic Meaning

In order to appreciate the kind of meaning dreams offer we have to move beyond the factual and literal to the symbolic. Most dreams are symbolic: that is, they point beyond themselves so that the meaning is not limited to what is seen. In terms of the three categories mentioned above, the kind of meaning given in most dreams is metaphorical rather than factual, multi-level rather than one-dimensional, and more subjective than objective. In the great majority of cases, they refer to the dreamer's own inner life. They put faces on different attitudes and identities that exist within our total personality. Rather than speaking in a directly factual way, they offer meaning on several different levels at the same time and give a different kind of meaning than facts do.

An example of the symbolic meaning of a dream is found in the case of Pharaoh's dream in Genesis 41. He dreamed that he stood by a river and seven fat cattle came up out of the river. After them, seven lean cattle came up out of the river and devoured the seven fat cattle. He awoke. After falling asleep again, he had a second dream in which seven ears of corn sprang up on one stalk, full and good. Then seven thin and wasted ears sprang up and devoured the seven good ears. The interpretation which was given to Joseph was that the two dreams had one meaning: there would be seven years of plenty followed by seven years of famine in the land. That the dream is repeated a second time in a slightly different form might indicate that it is of God and that it will happen soon, often an indication when something is doubled or twinned in a dream. The cattle and corn images are not far from the literal facts, but they are symbolic in that they represent the whole biological reality of food. The sevenness might symbolize the completeness of the effect. What we are saying here is that the language of dreams is symbolic rather than literal, and that the quality of symbolic meaning makes it metaphorical, multi-level and subjective.

From the discussion thus far, you may have the impression that dream interpretation is largely a matter of figuring out the personal messages that are there and applying them to life. There is a danger, however, in treating dreams like puzzles to be solved. Analyzing a dream as something to be thought through can have the effect of distancing us from it. *Thinking about* a dream objectifies it, much like hanging a picture on the wall, as something we can talk about or admire. Rather, the meaning of dreams is something we grasp best by experiencing it, like entering into the picture and feeling it as part of ourselves. Interpretation that is only analysis turns images into concepts. The kind of meaning that is given by the symbols and images of dreams is experienced by entering into, or *participating in*, symbols. Such participation turns images into experience and life process. We feel the images as part of ourselves. Strictly speaking, to unlock the meaning of a dream requires more than just interpretation: we need to live the dream. We will have more to say about participating in, or living, the dream symbols in the next chapter and in the practical method of dream work described in chapter 8.

Four Functions of Dreaming

Before ending this chapter on the meaning of dreams, it would be helpful to mention something about the purpose of dreams. Dreams appear to fulfil certain tasks in our personal psychological economy. Strictly speaking, it is not certain whether the dream actually accomplishes these functions itself, or if it is a reflection of some deeper process, which fulfils these functions and of which the dream is a by-product. Here I will describe the functions as if the dream itself played these roles.

A. Dreams process each day's experience.

Dreams often are responses to recent events in the dreamer's emotional life. Freud saw them as focused on the events of the previous day, while Jung extended that to include a broader time range. Dreaming may be seen as an attempt to integrate recent events, especially those that are emotionally charged, into the overall pattern of the dreamer's experience and self-concept. It represents the processing of experience both for self-understanding and the formulation of a response. The research experiments using red goggles, mentioned in the previous chapter, come to mind as an example of how dreams reflect the day's perceptions. Just as the color came through in the dreams of those subjects, so the emotional tones of the day come through our dreams.

B. Dreams integrate current experience with unresolved childhood issues.

Some dreams are concerned not only with coming to terms with events in one's recent life, but also with memories from childhood that we may associate with those events. Issues that were too difficult to resolve at the time remain as conflicts or complexes in the psyche and need to be reworked from the vantage point of adulthood. Such factors may lie behind a current dream. So we need to ask not only what relevance the dream might have to a situation we faced in the last day or so, but also how the dream may relate to an earlier situation. What could be the connection between the current situation and the earlier situation and how could the dream symbol be related to both? A woman dreamed of a polished wooden bureau in a traditional dining room which was bathed in warm afternoon sunlight. The previous day she had been viewing antique furniture similar to the bureau in her dream. Then she associated the warm wood with a piece of furniture in her mother's farmhouse and with an episode which had taken place near that bureau when she was young. An additional clue is that wood often has a symbolic connection to mother. In such a way, associations to dream images may lead back to childhood events.

Freud believed that dreams contained an early childhood wish, long past and buried, which he believed is seeking fulfilment in the present. As each day's experiences and thoughts distil into emotionally-toned patterns, certain associations may be established between something in that "day residue," as Freud called it, and the childhood wish, which may then be expressed in disguised form in a dream the following night. Because the wish may be too painful or forbidden to receive explicitly, it may have to be distorted or hidden in order to protect the dreamer. Many dreams may waken the dreamer because they are not well-enough disguised. Because some dreams may be touching on highly sensitive material that has been repressed for good reason and is being presented in edited form, as it were, by the dream, great respect needs to be shown to the pace at which a person is willing to explore his dreams. Meanings ought not be forced into conscious acceptance.

C. Dreams help in one's becoming.

Dreams not only serve to reconcile the developmental problems of one's life, but also help the person realize her possibilities and potentialities. This was one of Jung's greatest contributions—to see that the unconscious is not only filled with the skeletons of the past, but also is open to the future and its expansive possibilities. The psyche is set on a growth path in which the personality has opportunities every day to expand and develop in knowledge, accomplishment and relationships. Wholeness is the goal and this is assisted by dreams that make the unconscious available to consciousness. In this view, dreams are given in the service of self-healing and personal growth, so that the person may become all that she can be.

D. Dreams also express transpersonal growth.

Some dreams have meaning not only for the individual dreamer's life but for the race as a whole. We speak of such dreams as "transpersonal." Many primitive tribes recognize these as "big dreams" pertaining to the whole tribe or clan, and require it as the individual's duty to share them with the tribe. It could be as vital a matter as survival.

Dreams not only play a vital role in the individual's own developmental struggle, either with past influences or future potentials, but also contribute to the racial consciousness shared by all people. I have already mentioned Jung's dream of the map of Europe which foretold the extent of the bloodshed to come in the First World War, and thus had a relevance far beyond the individual. This is an instance of a much larger phenomenon in which dreams reflect a coming of wholeness to the consciousness of mankind. After exhaustive research lasting over ten years, Jung felt confident that he had found a basic symbol of wholeness which was universal among mankind. He used the Hindi word "mandala" to describe this symbol which was expressed in various circular forms and possessed a wholeness-making power. Present in the collective unconscious of humans, this circular symbol has emerged in various forms, from Aztec clocks to Hopi Indian medicine circles to halos. Jung thought that the mounting reports, from mid-century on, of UFO sightings were another instance of its expression. Such circular images in dreams may contribute not only to the individual's growth, but also may be part of humanity's movement to wholeness.

To speak in this way of symbols having a psychological effect or producing a spiritual movement, raises the question of the role of symbols in dreams, to which we turn now.

5
THE POWER OF SYMBOLS

Symbols exert a great influence in everyday life. A woman novelist was speaking of how she coped with the hard, hard work of writing. "I imagine as I sit down to write that I am strapping myself into a space capsule for a marvellous flight into outer space. I'm tremendously excited about what I'm going to discover as I prepare to blast off!" Obviously, the symbol of a space capsule combined for her the sense of power, propulsion and exploration. But these are far more than flat ideas or empty concepts. There she was, still seated at her desk, but through imagination was filled with the energy of that space craft symbol.

Symbols in dreams have the same effect. When we first wake up and the dream is fresh upon us, there is often a mood or energy that the symbols of the dream cast over us. That same energy can be felt later when we recall the dream and reenter the aura of its symbols. The man who, as a boy suffering wartime rationing in Europe, dreamed of the jars of cooking oil and woke up with the full expectation of them actually being in his backyard (see pp. 9–10), provides a good example. The attitude of expectancy, the feeling which told him how very much he would value such a luxurious commodity, possessed him as he awoke. It was as charging to his emotions as if he had actually tasted it.

A symbol is a representation of a relatively unknown fact to which it makes a bridge or connection. It is much more than a sign that merely points like a highway sign to a certain destination. We become involved in what the symbol represents. By saying that symbols represent a relatively unknown fact, we mean that symbols go beyond what we are conscious of and make us able to experience it. A symbol expresses a largely unconscious element which "grasps" us.

Through symbols we actually participate in the reality it represents. Take the symbol of a school mascot, for example. Wallace Clift illustrates this participatory nature of symbols by saying that for loyal faculty and students, an attack on a school mascot is an attack on the school itself.[14] The mascot represents the unseen feelings, memories and values that students and faculty attach to the school. The attitude taken toward that mascot by others is taken personally, as if the person were somehow feeling the feelings of the mascot.

Participation in a symbol brings the unseen reality to life, like a person who has read about a foreign country but then actually travels there. He come to "know" it—its villages, terrain and climate; its architecture, industry and buildings; its smells, its colors; its customs, its people, and the sounds of its streets. All of this is present when he hears its name and he is "there" again.

That is what dreams do. Dreams speak in the language of symbols. Through symbols—the images and stories—dreams allow us to enter an unknown world. We may have supposed that that world was merely a world of flat pictures. In fact, it is not pictures, but energy. Through symbols, the reality of the unconscious becomes alive for us. Through the symbol, we experience the energy of realities that are beyond us. A symbol such as a spider, for example, has certain meanings which may be conscious to the average person—that of poison, of the female killing its mate, or of entrapment of victims in its web. We may actually feel these aspects of the spider and shudder.

As well, there are aspects of the spider symbol which may be unconscious, for example, that it has a lunar (feminine) aspect, that it spins its web out of itself, and that it has the archetypal identity of the life-weaver. These aspects of the spider symbol may also become conscious and thus permit us to experience energy and meanings which we did not previously have of the spider. Its circular web might give a sense of the infinite process of wholeness, the ordering and holding pattern of life, and its spinning might suggest the creative order behind nature. In such complex ways, symbols serve not only to permit communication of various conscious meanings that are intangible or multi-levelled, but also to connect consciousness to the unconscious and its contents.

In this latter process of connecting us to the unconscious, dreams are paramount. Coming as they do from the unconscious, dreams convey in symbolic form the outline of meanings which lie beyond our normal understanding in the unknown depths of the psyche.

According to Jung, basic psychological reality may be divided into instinct and image. Instinct refers to the raw energy of the psyche, while images offer a meaningful focus for that energy. When symbolic images are expressed in a dream, a way is being provided by the unconscious by which instinctual energy may be directed and shaped into meaningful forms. Hope is an example: hope awakens an energy which attaches to the image hoped for. Hope has to have an image for which to strive. It believes that a certain situation will come to pass or that a promised result will be fulfilled. Hope without an image to hope for does not exist.

The underlying principle—and this is basic to all that follows—is that *energy follows the image*. As Jung says: "The psychological mechanism that transforms energy is the symbol."[15] Symbols are what Wallace Clift calls "channelizers of psychic energy."[16] They provide a form by which energy can be conveyed. This may be illustrated by the biblical story of the woman with a hemorrhage who came to Jesus in the crowd and said to herself: "If only I may touch his garment, I shall be whole" (Matthew 9:21). The image of touching Jesus' garment and then being well brought the energy of healing. "Your faith has made you well," is Jesus' evaluation, showing that, although he felt power flowing out of him, it was accessed by her faith in him. The energy follows the image.

I worked with a talented man who was stuck in inertia, unable to focus himself to effective action. He would be easily diverted from essential work into playing games with his children, or being distracted around the house, while the hours and days slipped by fruitlessly. I suggested that he visualize an animal that would represent himself and he came up with the unicorn. I pressed him for something that wasn't imaginary and he had great difficulty seeing himself as an actual animal or bird. Could he see himself as a stallion? He admitted he really couldn't. The image he had, the unicorn, drew on the idealism, the high level of purity and refinement, of this man, but it also expressed his lack of reality and absence of practical day-to-day application. What he needed was an image, like a lion, that would empower him for living in this world.

The difference a symbol can make in one's energy level was brought home to me by the following dream which I had. It came at a time near the beginning of my analysis when I was groping for direction.

In the dream I am water-skiing on the blue-green waters of the Caribbean on a beautiful sunny day. I let the skiis go and slip down into the water. Underwater I can see the sandy bottom 30 or 40 feet down. The water is crystal clear. I see a log cottage sitting on the bottom and I swim down to investigate. The cottage interests me and I go through it. It has a "For Sale" sign at the front and I notice a woman some distance away at a well. She is a domestic woman, strong and able-bodied, with a bandana around her head. She is drawing water out of the well with a bucket. I ask her about the cottage, saying that I want to buy it. She tells me to talk to my brother-in-law (who is actually in real estate) who knows all about it. I swim to the surface and see a great ocean freighter going by and find my skis. I awoke with a sense of enthusiasm.

In working with the dream, my analyst identified the woman as a representation of the water-bearer archetype, a familiar image in legend and literature. He remarked that she was a very important resource for me—someone I should get to know—and the fact that she was drawing water from below the bottom of the ocean indicated the deep spiritual reality within me. As the meaning sank in and I resonated to the figure of the water-drawer, I sensed an energy flooding up in me with great excitement.

Sometimes people are unable to access the energy of an image because they insist on limiting the meaning to the factual and real, and by that they mean the material world. A patient, who was greatly in need of love and affirmation and who initially wanted me, as therapist, to supply that love, came in time to have a series of dreams in which men appeared who held her and expressed their desire for her. Evidently, her unconscious was producing dreams to fill the void in her life; but her angry, disappointed response was that they weren't "real" arms, because they were "only" dreams. She wasn't willing to accept the symbolic transformation being offered. Because she equated reality with the physical world, the lover in her dreams seemed unreal and she experienced no fulfilment. If we contrast her with the "astronaut" writer with which we began, we can easily see the different energy that comes when a person accepts and participates in a symbol.

Symbolic thinking requires imagination enough to depart from the literal. "To be born again" (John 3:3) can be taken literally, as Nicodemus did, or symbolically, as Jesus did. If you think carnally, you will be flesh. Think symbolically and you will be spirit (vs. 6). A symbol, then, is a bridge between two worlds: those who remain literal and stay stuck on the level of material satisfaction never cross the bridge to experience the power of the unconscious, nor to live what faith can produce.

It is a matter of imagination. What is imaged needs to be so real that it is feasible for the person to let go to the symbol, that is, to participate in its reality. Like the novelist-cum-astronaut, it means catching the excitement of seeing where it leads.

Where it leads is to networks of associated meanings and shades of meaning. Edward Edinger, a noted Jungian analyst and scholar, has studied certain symbols, in depth, and the various meanings which gather around them like an extended family. He has charted the way in which meanings associate with a central symbol and then extend, through associations, to other meanings in an almost endless fashion. To illustrate how a symbol spins out a whole web of interconnected meanings, let us consider a study Edinger[17] did of one symbol, quicklime. He remarks how, historically, quicklime has been known for its unique property of growing hot when water is added, unlike other compounds that are cooled by water. Consequently, it was believed that it possessed an inner energy whose possibilities intrigued ancients.

For this reason, quicklime came to have a potent number of associations. Tracing some of these through Edinger's chart, we find various lines of movement out from this simple image of quicklime toward resolution and fulfillment. A few of the many developing lines of related meanings which he traces are associations that go from quicklime to ash to mourning to death; from quicklime to ash to whiteness to redemption; and another from quicklime to hell to guilt to repentance to redemption.

Other lines of associations will further suggest the richness of the symbol, how subtle the connections can be to related meanings and yet how far they can lead in transforming experience:

quicklime-fire-sulphur-purgatory-cleansing-solution in water;
quicklime-fire-concupiscence-desire-blood-baptism-solution in water;
quicklime-fire-ethereal fire-Holy Spirit-Logos tongue-inspiration-sublime being;
quicklime-a test, ordeal or judgment-Divine wrath-slaying-death;
quicklime-refining extractor-separation.

These lines of association, which are only a sample of available associations, reflect the myriad experiences humans have had which relate to quicklime and hint at how the psyche has understood the various connections. Edinger is a master at formulating similar charts of other major symbols.

Of course, we are all constantly doing the same thing in

one degree or another. Our minds must be crisscrossed with similar charts of related understandings, some shared by humanity and others uniquely our own. What is thought but some form of meaningful connection between the experiences and concepts of our life, and education but learning how to balance the relationships of life in a beneficial way? A strong case can be made for the primary importance of verbal skills in that process; but an even stronger case might favor the basic role of image-making. We abbreviate explanations and encapsulate experience in the form of symbols. They are compressed life experience, values in picture form. This is how our mind at its depths works—through the minting and exchanging of symbols.

If in our formation, as we develop understanding and mastery of experience in the world, symbols compress experience, then there might also be a time when the reverse is true and the symbol makes its compressed meanings available, unlocks, as it were, its treasures. The symbol, therefore, opens up many possibilities of interpretation, each meaning having its own energy. One could, by keeping a record of dream symbols, cumulating or recurring, over a period of time, find a pattern in one's dreams which might reveal a direction and psychological development.

A Format for Dream Analysis

6
HOW TO RECORD AND KEEP YOUR DREAMS

1. Remembering Dreams

Everyone dreams:
The trick is in remembering them

Time pressure and work schedules are often problems for those wanting to remember their dreams. On weekdays, the average person is thrust abruptly into a waking world where there is no time for reflection. Most people are jarred awake by alarms and pressed immediately into a conscious whirl of activity. If this is your pattern, then perhaps you need to examine your priorities. If you don't have time to recall, much less to reflect on, your dreams, perhaps you are too busy. Taking time, even a few well-chosen minutes, indicates a healthy self-respect and a willingness to nurture yourself. Once your interest is excited by what is happening in your dreams it is amazing how much easier it is to find the time, even in very demanding schedules.

More difficult again is the stress of rotating shift work which may upset regular rhythms and break up consistent patterns of sleep. Similarly, those whose sleep is disturbed by having to tend to the needs of an infant or an ill family member may need special encouragement to monitor their dreams. They need to be assured that their efforts at recalling dreams will be well-rewarded.

Sometimes there is a tendency to be discouraged if less than a complete dream is remembered. It is important not to devalue partial dreams or fragments because of some such perfectionistic ideal. Fragments of dreams and even single images can be very useful. Many times I've had the experience that a person will mention in passing an image or brief snatch of a dream that they regarded as not worth considering and that tiny bit of a dream will open up to very large meanings that totally surprised the person.

Hints at stimulating the dream recall

Don't wake up suddenly to an alarm. The sudden focusing on the waking world can dislodge the memory of a dream. Let yourself come out of sleep naturally and gradually. On the other hand, don't let the dream state you have been in become blurred or muddied by the intrusion of waking thoughts over a long period of waking up. Sleep studies show that the longer a person takes to awaken the less likely the dream will be remembered and the more likely it will be in a "thinking" rather than a "feeling" mode. It seems that we edit the material in our dreams into a more reasonable form the longer we have to process it as we awaken. We may even distance ourself from it by altering parts of it or not remembering it.

To assist recall, it is important that the dream memory be crystallized as soon as possible. That can be done by simply going over it in your mind. Having just wakened up, or as you are in the twilight between sleep and awake, focus on what you may have been dreaming. Fix on any image that you recall in the dream and tell yourself that image, for example, a puppy dog, a red beach ball. If possible, write that down as soon as you can, and later, when you have time to recover the whole dream, you can go back to that single image and pull the rest of the dream back by means of it, like pulling on the end of a rope. Of course, the best system is to write the dream down in full within minutes of rising; but the time pressures of most people's work lives make that difficult. Getting the "bare bones" of the dream in an image or brief story outline may be the only way of holding onto the dream until you have time to record it in full. Even a dozen words jotted down in thirty seconds may be enough to bring the whole dream back later in the day.

By emphasizing how much you want to recall your dreams, you may help yourself to be aware of dreaming while you are actually dreaming, like a "mind-over" the dream observing the dream. This is called "lucid dreaming" and is usually not controllable. One client, who had been frustrated by not having dreams, came one day to tell me triumphantly he had had a dream and in the midst of it he cried out to himself, "Good, now I'll have something to tell Dr. Slater."

Believe that you will recall your dreams. That may sound foolish, but in fact many people begin by being skeptical about the reality of dreams and the unconscious, and their doubt or lack of focus has a dampening effect. Believing that you will recall a dream is important as you are preparing for sleep or even next morning, after you have moved into your daily activities, because a positive mental attitude assists one's natural processes. Such an attitude may be enhanced by making a verbal affirmation to yourself: I am going to remember my dream when I wake up in the morning, or I am going to remember that dream I had last night. Often a person will be surprised during the day to have a dream come to memory which hadn't registered in any way previously, except that you knew you had had a dream.

Ask yourself for dreams. As you go to sleep, fix your mind on a question you want answered, or a problem to be solved. Feel how much you want an answer. Imagine what it would be like to have it solved.

Pray for dreams. Some people who have faith in God are timid about asking something for themselves. They may think of themselves as being "selfish" if they ask for a dream or a solution to a problem. Perhaps that attitude explains why they receive so little by way of dreams. If dreams come to enable them to grow to be more mature, effective people, how could that be selfish in any morally inferior sense? "Ask, and it will be given you" is a central teaching of Jesus' Sermon on the Mount.

Find another person with whom you can share your dreams, if you are comfortable with that. It must be someone who can be trusted, who is a good listener and whom you feel understands you. It is difficult to understand our own dreams, we are so close to them, and they often are just a little bit out of our own reach. Having such a person listen and reflect on our dreams, gives an objectivity which helps interpretation. It also aids in stimulating the remembering of dreams. There is an expectancy when you know someone will be there to share the dream with you.

2. Recording Dreams

Recording dreams is almost as important as recalling them

There is no substitute for writing a dream down as soon as you waken. While it is fresh in your memory, the details flow more easily and the feelings of the dream are still close at hand. Even if the dream wakens you in the middle of the night, write it down. Keeping pen and notebook on the night-stand provides ready access and eliminates delay. Some people prefer using a small cassette recorder which minimizes any disturbance and permits them to remain in bed while recording the dream.

Keep a pad and pen by your bedside to jot down a dream as soon as you awaken. Don't allow yourself to be fooled by the vividness of a dream into thinking that you will certainly be able to remember it later. Write it down while it is fresh and clear. Dreams have a way of slipping back into unconsciousness, or of being edited by the conscious mind, soon after waking. This is especially true of dreams that awaken a person in the night. Write it down immediately, even the main features of a dream will provide the clues to recall the whole dream in the morning light.

Journalling is a valuable method of charting and assisting personal growth. This simply requires keeping a notebook in which you enter a daily log of your reflections on your life. Recording your dreams in the midst of your regular journal is a good way to integrate the inner and outer aspects of your life's journey. It also helps to put the dream in context of other factors in your daily life and experience.

Some people find that recording their dreams on a small audiotape is an easy way to keep them, and they find it quicker than writing in the morning rush. If you are fortunate, you could make use of a personal secretary: One participant in a dream seminar told me she had found the answer to recording her dreams. Previously she found that her dreams fled when she opened her eyes. "Now," she said, "I lie there very still when I first wake up, with my eyes closed tight, and I whisper (her husband's name) and he writes down what I tell him."

3. Some Factors That Hinder Dreaming

It is well known that alcohol and certain drugs have an inhibiting or distorting effect on dreaming. Similarly, being too extraverted, overworked or fatigued take a toll on dreaming. Frequently a person will experience periods when dreams dry up, when normally they dream regularly. It may be that they have been too busy in their outer life for dreams to be considered; or they may have enough conscious material to process without adding more from the unconscious. The kind of excessive time-pressured living that many modern people get caught up in typically does not allow room for the inner world to speak.

But perhaps the most serious hindrance is a negative attitude: having little or no expectation of one's dreams, and not paying attention to dream-messages, may undermine the process. Edward Whitmont, a gifted analyst and interpreter of Jung, wrote: "The unconscious relates to the conscious personality in a manner which corresponds to the way this conscious standpoint itself approaches or fails to relate to the unconscious."[18] In short, the unconscious responds in kind to the conscious attitude, whether positive or negative.

This brings up a most important factor in working with dreams. One's self-esteem is often crucial to a healthy use of dreams. It takes a strong ego to interact effectively with the unconscious. That strength is evident in being able to have a positive, expectant attitude toward the unconscious, as Whitmont describes, but also toward one's conscious ego. It is necessary for the person to have a good enough sense of herself to know what is real and what is unreal. Before delving into the meaning of one's dreams, it is highly advisable to spend some time building up one's ego and confirming one's own truth. This may be helped through a process of affirming one's strengths and worth, learning to make realistic decisions and to take responsibility, and in having mutually supportive relationships.

7
WORKING WITH THE IMAGES AND SYMBOLS IN DREAMS

As we attempt to analyze a dream we must recognize that the dream is a living thing and cannot be made into an object for study. Its meaning comes out in relationship to the dreamer's consciousness and grows as it is integrated into the dreamer's life. The dream is part of the dreamer's psychic process, like a snapshot of a river flowing, and needs to be put in that framework of a constantly evolving life. It is located in a moment in that life-flow and gains its significance in relation to the surrounding flow. That includes the events of daily life which surround it and with which it may be in dialogue.

But the meaning of the dream also involves the interpretation process itself. The dream, once landed in consciousness, has its second life, as it were, in the development that takes place through the various connections that are made to the dreamer's inner and outer worlds. It matters, therefore, when the dream is processed and in what circumstances. The intuition or perception of the moment in which it is received and studied are part of its meaning. The dream lives again and grows further in such moments of conscious participation.

In providing the format of dream analysis which follows, I want to respect this dynamic sense of the dream. Any attempt to hold it down into these categories of analysis is like a stop-action of a waterfall and will be artificial. These categories should be viewed only as a means by which the dream may grasp the dreamer. The dream must be lived.

Normally, there are four parts to doing dream analysis: the Content, the Context, the Associations, and Amplification.

The *content* includes everything that is actually given in the dream itself, the setting, all the images, any story or narrative, the basic theme, action and outcome, and the feelings involved.

The *context* comprises whatever emotional events preceded and followed the dreaming of the dream, including events and issues of the preceding day, together with the dreamer's feelings on waking.

Associations refer to any or all memories, thoughts or feelings which come in response to any individual part of the dream or to the dream as a whole.

Amplification is the process of allowing or assisting the meaning of various images or symbols to develop more fully. Dreams tend to disguise meanings by compressing them into symbols which are ambiguous. A major part of dream interpretation involves drawing out such meanings until they are full-bodied and recognizable. Only then can a dreamer sift out the meanings which best apply.

The Content

1. The Setting

Often the first words of a dream give its reference meaning: "I was wandering in the fog at night..." or "I was climbing a steep cliff and holding on for dear life when...." suggest right away what kind of circumstance the dream may be addressing in the dreamer's life. The "fog" or the "cliff" may be metaphors for lostness or danger.

The setting may be a place that indicates in a general way what the dream is about: "We were in a mall or huge complex..." (which I often find may be a symbol of one's actual complex or psychological wound). It may be a place that has a special function: "I was in a school classroom..." or "I was in a hospital operating room..." which may identify that function or task as significant. Or it may be a place that is familiar to the dreamer and has certain personal meanings: "We were gathered in grandma's bedroom." (Perhaps a childhood memory being addressed.) Some settings, such as buildings, factories and machinery, because they are man-made, may indicate a memory or complex that formed under some human conflict, while natural settings may express what is "given" genetically or is being worked through with relative freedom now. Whether the setting is a house (suggesting perhaps something about the dreamer's own life or body) or is an institutional public building (indicating perhaps a collective rather than individual reference) may also be significant.

Although the setting may be associated with some experience of the previous day, it may also refer back to some earlier, childhood place. If, for example, the setting is a house familiar to one's childhood, the question is twofold: what happened in that house that the dream may be addressing, and what happened yesterday that brought that memory back? The nature of symbols is to constantly bridge between similar experiences across one's life.

2. The Images

What are the actual animals, objects, persons, or scenes? What designs, shapes or forms are depicted? Note any special colors or lack of color. All of these constitute the symbols of a dream, which can have both personal and collective meaning.

The images of a dream represent the way energy is taking form within the psyche. One can feel the difference between energy that is symbolized in the images of persons or animals, and that which is in inanimate forms, such as trees or rivers or mountains, and that which forms into stone or man-made images such as concrete buildings or a machine such as a bulldozer. The contrast here between a building and a bulldozer raises a matter that will come up again, namely the activity or power (or lack of) embodied in an object or image.

3. The Main Theme

However involved a dream may be, there is usually a common thread that runs through it. Try to express the main idea or purpose of the dream in a simple, one-sentence synopsis. Although, in the case of some dreams, it may seem almost too simple to state the theme, the significance of it may not become apparent until it is stated.

A woman once came to our first session with a dream which she had dreamed the previous night which had four distinct parts. At that time, it was very difficult to see any connection between them and if pressed to state a main theme all she might have said was that she had had a dream in which four different vignettes or views were presented. However, in the three years we then worked together in her analysis, it became quite clear that that original dream was laying out the four basic issues that she had to deal with in her analysis. Then the theme could be stated as "these four cameos show the struggles of my life."

Where the content of a dream does not involve a story or action sequence, the theme may be to portray a scene, a relationship, an image or a feeling.

4. *The Action or Effect*

Where there are events taking place as in a story sequence, observe the effect or outcome of the action. Is there a movement, a resolution, in the dream? What is accomplished in the dream? Attention to the action or movement taking place within a dream will often reveal where the energy is flowing (or blocked). Energy flow may also be evident when persons or materials are transformed in a dream. For example, when one person is replaced by another during a dream or when a substance changes state, as in a fire, explosion or chemical reaction, it may indicate a shift of energy or attitude within the psyche of the dreamer. The death of a person in a dream is a clear indication of energy going out of that symbol. One needs to ask where the energy or value that resided in that person has gone. Frequently another form will be assumed by something new appearing as a transformation of that energy, for example, a baby might be born or a new relationship begun in a dream. Babies often symbolize new beginnings.

5. *The Feeling Tone*

A key to understanding our dreams lies in noting the feeling tone in the dream; that is, while you were dreaming the dream what were your emotions? This will normally be the feelings of the dreamer. The feelings of other characters in the dream are important, too, and may be noted as expressions of attitudes that might be quite different than those held consciously by the dreamer. The dreamer's own feelings are helpful, both in relation to the feelings of others in the dream and in contrast to the dreamer's waking feelings.

Although I have spoken of feelings here in terms of emotion, the more important factor is to identify the feelings in the dream in terms of the worth that is attached to certain persons or objects. What are the feelings of value present in the dream?

The Context

6. *The Feeling on Waking*

Often the contrast between the conscious and unconscious minds will be felt as the dreamer emerges from a dream into consciousness. It may be a sense of great relief, if the dream has been frightening, to discover it was only a dream. Whether comforting or not, the felt difference between the attitude in the dream and the conscious attitude is of great importance. It makes a person aware of the range of his own attitudes and may indicate that an attitude different from the conscious attitude is emerging into consciousness and there may be a need to integrate the two by a shift in consciousness. Insofar as the felt difference between the feeling on waking and the feeling in the dream represents the challenge to accept new contents into consciousness, holding it in consciousness may be met with resistance and the dream might be forgotten as a way of avoiding the challenge of facing the feeling difference.

7. *Previous Day's Events*

Freud believed that dreams responded to the previous day's events. Jung, while not so narrowly focused, regarded dreams as the dialogue which the unconscious carries on with the conscious mind, usually in the light of recent events. He viewed the human mind as a self-regulating mechanism in which the unconscious seeks to bring balance, healing and wholeness to conciousness.

The context of a dream, then, would take in the whole

emotional, relational life of the person prior to the dream
and would be just as important to understanding the
significance of a dream as a witness' testimony is at a trial.
The events of the previous day or so, especially those that
had a priority impact on the dreamer, could be relevant.

8. Emotional Landscape

Any particular problems, stresses or emotionally
charged thoughts of the dreamer similarly would be
important to consider. Had the dreamer been seeking a
solution to a problem or specific need? What had been
the most important relational focus just prior to the
dream?

Equally, the emotional landscape includes emotionally
charged issues either before or after the actual dream.
Dreams may be in response to, or in anticipation of, such
issues that claim one's emotional attention. All of this
addresses the context to which the dream might be
speaking. Establishing the connection of the dream to the
surrounding conscious experience of the person is of
major importance in interpreting a dream.

Associations

Associations are anything that comes to mind in
connection with a dream or its parts. However foolish or
irrelevant they may seem to our conscious mind, they
have their own way of relating to a dream. Therefore, it is
important to note any associations you have to anything
in your dream, however unreasonable or absurd they may
seem. So-called stray thoughts or images often make a
very definite connection once we let them flow.

9. What associations do you have to any of the images in the dream?

10. What in your life is similar to elements in the dream?

11. What memories does the dream bring back?

12. What similarities does this dream have to other dreams you've had? To religious or secular stories, legends or fairytales?

Amplification

In the process of making the dream material more fully conscious, it is necessary to expand the message which has been compressed in the dream symbols. Meaning that is held in the unconscious is communicated through dreams in the form of symbols which partially hide its true meaning from consciousness. Disguised in this way, in the form of symbols, the messages are partial, ambiguous and fragmented. In order to be understood and received into consciousness, the meaning needs to be drawn out or amplified. The following are some methods of amplification.

13. Balance

The unconscious may be seeking to compensate the conscious attitude or situation according to a principle of balance. How is the dream different from my waking attitude or values? Here it is helpful to compare the feeling or attitude in the dream (#5) with the feeling on waking (#6). Reentering consciousness after a dream often brings the awareness of how different the two worlds are.

The contrast may be instructive in a variety of ways: the unconscious position as expressed in dream symbols and experienced by the dreamer as a particular attitude or feeling may be offering a potential way of growth, or suggesting a helpful adjustment, if adopted into one's conscious life. Take, for example, the born-again Christian who lived a moral life and was shocked to wake up from dreams in which murders and violence were an accepted commonplace. When these violent crimes, usually against men, became the theme of recurrent dreams, she began to ask what that very different attitude in her unconscious might mean. Studying the contrast led her to realize how completely she had repressed her anger about her former husband and how she had to acknowledge that anger consciously before she could go forward with her life. As she began to claim those angry feelings, she became aware that the difficulty went beyond her relationship with her former husband. She saw that in her relationships, in general, she had been self-effacing and timid about confronting others with her true feelings. The dreams were leading her to balance her former inhibited way of relating with a more forthright self-expression.

The unconscious often functions in dreams to show us the dark side of ourselves, that part of our personality that is opposite to our usual conscious position. In this way, it seeks to add to, enrich or adjust our conscious attitude. A good question, to ask, therefore, in analyzing a dream is: What does this dream correct or add to my usual way of living or thinking?

14. Active Imagination

In waking life, go back into the dream and dialogue with any of the persons in the dream with whom you feel comfortable. It is quite possible to enter into a discussion with these dream figures and to become familiar with them. Ask them whatever you wish and be prepared to have them ask you, too. Learn to wait and listen.

Caution: It may be unwise to open yourself in this way to evil or dangerous characters. Let your feelings be the guide. Don't force yourself to face figures that terrify you.

Active imagination is a potent exercise. To avoid slipping too deeply into the unconscious, it is important that you not do active imagination when you are alone. Arrange to have a friend present who can remind you of the real world to which you belong.

15. Gestalt

This refers to the ability to see things in different perspectives and thus have a sense of the whole. The dreamer, or "dream-ego," normally stands for that part of the unconscious that is most closely like the conscious personality. However, other parts of the unconscious personality may be present in the dream in other symbols. All characters, animals and objects in a dream may express different aspects of the dreamer. Allow yourself to be any of the objects in the dream and feel into those various identities. What is their point of view? How am I like the persons, animals or object in the dream?

Making a mask which represents a character in one's dream can be an effective way of getting in touch with the meaning embodied in that dream character. There is a great value in the process of creating the mask itself; in conceiving it, shaping and forming it. Even if it is only a paper bag with eyes, mouth and nose cut out and colored with crayons or markers, it is a work of intuition and imagination, which connects with the unconscious from which the dream flowed. Usually insights and feelings begin to flow as one works on the mask itself. More elaborate creations can involve papier-mâché or plaster of paris materials. Then in the putting on and wearing of the mask the dreamer steps into the role more completely and may experience the energy and inner reality of that dream character. After working through the feelings evoked by the mask, a dreamer may want to keep the mask and display it as a reminder of that meaning and the reality it has as a part of the dreamer's life.

Acting out one's dream in a group format as a kind of psychodrama can be a particularly powerful form of gestalt. It requires, however, having a willing group of participants or friends who will allow your meanings to emerge and not impose their own.

16. Draw or sculpt the dream images

Drawing, painting or sculpting images or whole scenes from a dream can be a helpful exercise. In this way, images become more concrete and may expand in their richness; and relationships between participants and objects in the dream may become more clear. Forget artistic values for the moment and focus instead on giving a reflective, even meditative, expression to the images, shapes and characters in the dream. As the images take shape, they may come alive with their own meaning and begin to reveal connections which had been hidden. In this way, a dream may continue to unfold its meaning.

17. Confront your monster

Dreams such as nightmares, where monsters or terror presents itself, may be offering the opportunity of coming to terms with some deep fear. Facing that terror in active imagination may help it to transform. Giving the monster a friendly name, asking what its purpose is in your life, or telling it that you want to be friends, may serve to integrate it and free that energy for more constructive purposes. This is the practice of the Dream People of Malaysia who teach their children to do precisely these things in confronting dream monsters, believing that the monster symbolizes a part of reality which they need to befriend and win over.

In view of the caution noted above (#14), a good test is to ask yourself if you are willing to risk confrontation in each particular case and get your gut reaction. It may make a difference if you confront that dream personage when you are in the safety of a therapy relationship or with a trusted friend.

18. What question might this dream be answering?

Since a dream may be understood as a response to one's conscious life, daily experience is often the setting to which a dream speaks. A dream may sometimes be seen as an answer to a conscious question or problem, or a comment on one's situation in life, or a form of questioning or warning about some conscious decision or action. One way of trying to assist the process of dreaming is to ask a question before falling asleep at night. Whether that is put explicitly or not, a person's life may frequently be seen as expressing a question or need. A dream may be a visible answer to such questions.

19. Intervention

When working with dreams of danger, perplexity or abandonment, invite a religious figure such as Jesus or a trusted friend to come into your dream. Using active imagination, see that figure in your dream and watch what he or she does with the situation.

A woman, who had suffered sexual and verbal abuse from two husbands and other trusted men and was subject to severe depression, told me her dream of a huge scorpion that came after her. Instead of stinging her, it exploded all over her face and neck. Telling the dream, she was almost sick with her terror of scorpions. Because

she had already indicated her Christian faith to me, I
suggested that she ask Jesus to come into the scene and
for her simply to observe what he did. Almost at once,
she saw him come into the dream scene of the scorpion
which had just exploded over her. She saw him turn and
come to her, gently wipe the scorpion pieces from her
face and then take her by the hand. There was a
noticeable calming following that encounter and, as she
opened her eyes again, she felt strengthened within
herself.

20. Completion

How does the dream end? Some dreams are incomplete
and need an ending, others end in ways that are terrifying
or troubling. What resolution or completion would you
like to see to the dream? What completion can you believe
is possible or likely? As in active imagination, go back into
the dream, in a waking state, and imagine the ending you
would like or the one that seems to fit at that time.

A man who was facing financial cutbacks, and who
usually dealt with life by denying his feelings and
thinking his way through, had a dream in which he was
carrying a young boy on his shoulders just as a sixty-foot
dinosaur turned toward him. As he looked in terror, he
saw that the dinosaur was not real. It was like the toy
model his son played with that was made of strips of
interlocking wood. But it was sixty feet long and as he
looked its neck moved and its great head swooped down
toward them. In sheer terror he ran with the boy on his
shoulders to find some place to hide from the monster
that was pursuing them. Somehow he knew that the
monster could not attack if someone saw him. He took
refuge in a betting shop where a friendly man behind the
counter welcomed him. The man knew all about the
dinosaur but wasn't the least bit afraid. The dreamer

asked why the man wasn't afraid and he said, "There's nothing to be afraid of. He's inside you." The dreamer went over to the window of the shop and looked out to see where the dinosaur was, as the dream ended.

Later, in working on the dream, the man realized that the dinosaur represented his fears of financial woe. He also recognized that the betting shop indicated the need to take some calculated risks in facing his fears. He set about making a plan of action in dealing with his financial situation and a list of alternative outcomes, if the worst happened. Then, in active imagination, he reentered the dream scene to talk with the betting shop man. What could he do to overcome the dinosaur? "Just face him." Still carrying the boy on his shoulders the man stepped out of the door, looked squarely at the dinosaur who still stood there, and in a loud voice he shouted, "Go away!" To his astonishment a shudder went through the dinosaur. It began to tremble and shake and then collapsed on the ground like a pile of matchsticks.

21. Archetypal identity

Many of the symbols in dreams give expression to our complexes, those unique bundles of experience marking our fears, conflicts, dependencies, and distorted views of reality. Each complex corresponds to and is rooted in an underlying healing image, called an archetype. (Archetypes and complexes will be explained in more detail in chapter 9.) The personal mother complex, for example, is rooted in the Great Mother archetype, the ego is rooted in the Self archetype. The collective unconscious has the ability to produce symbols from its depths which are able to reconcile and transcend the distortions and conflicts of the complexes. This ability is called the "transcendent function" whereby complexes and conflicts are not denied but outgrown and integrated into a larger whole.

In doing dream work, it is essential that archetypal symbols be recognized and responded to consciously. They usually manifest with power, clarity and wholeness; there may be a sense of breakthrough, the resolution of conflict or emergence into freedom. Paramount among archetypes is the Self which may be expressed in symbols of wholeness, such as mandala (magical circle) forms, a wonder child, or divine figure. Note any archetypal symbols or feelings that accompany archetypal expression and observe the effect on the symbols which express your complexes.

22. New Knowledge

Those who work regularly with dreams know that there is a purpose to our dreaming. Something is being revealed that we need to bring into consciousness. We can assume that every dream contains some new message that we have not previously heard or acted upon. What does it tell me about myself or others that I did not know before? What does this dream add to my understanding?

23. Conscious Response

The focus of the foregoing analysis is to form a conscious response to the dream. On the basis of all that has been gleaned from each of the various categories covered, what action, question or decision do you make in response to the dream? If dreams truly offer to add to our knowledge, then it is important that we carry that knowledge forward to some beneficial result. Make a decision, do something, in response to the dream. Not to act on a dream that has given a clear message is to discourage further dialogue.

You may need time to digest the import of a dream.

Sometimes it helps to distance from it for a day or two. Then, on returning, it may be seen with more objectivity and perspective. Also, dreams are seen in different light when put in the context of a series of dreams, where repeating themes and symbols may form meaningful connections. Furthermore, when one has moved forward in time and then goes back and reviews dreams that occurred sometime in the past, there may be fresh nuances and connections because the dreamer has moved further on in understanding. In short, one can continue to reflect on past dreams and to formulate a fuller response.

Rarer Images

Some elements are not as commonly found in dreams as others. In my experience, the occurrence of puns and of images of parts of the human body or organs are fairly rare. For that reason, these are not included in the regular worksheet format. Nevertheless, they can play an important role in some dreams and should not be overlooked when they do occur.

24. Puns

The meaning of a dream may also be conveyed by a pun or an absurdity. In my experience, these are not very frequent and when they do occur we are more likely to stumble upon them accidentally or have them pointed out by another person than to decode them ourselves. It does help to let your imagination go free in stating any sayings or near-word likenesses that connect with the dream.

A favorite example is that of the woman who dreamed that a woman friend was helping her take her woollen sweater off by pulling it over her head. She could not make any associations to it until it was pointed out to her that the real meaning might be in the pun that the friend was "pulling the wool over her eyes" in a certain relationship she had. It "clicked" with her that this indeed was the message of the dream.

25. Body References

There is evidence that dreams are connected not only with our minds and emotions, but also with our bodies. In research at the University of Michigan, Bob Smith found that there was a connection between different outcomes from surgery and the kinds of dreams the patients had. Those who did well in surgery tended to have normal dreams before, during and after recovery from surgery. Those who did poorly in coming through surgery tended to have dreams before, during and after recovery from surgery which focused on death (male patients) and on separation (female patients). Those who died in surgery had seldom dreamed or had a few meaningless dreams prior to surgery. This is part of a growing body of evidence that suggests that dreams may reflect our bodily state.

Some dreams will have reference to parts of the body and may refer specifically to one's health. When you dream of an organ or part of your body that is not well, it may be wise to have it checked out medically. In 1983, when I was taking a course in cancer self-help education from Stephanie Simonton, coauthor of *Getting Well Again*, I asked her about her experience with dreams in working with cancer patients. She told our group that earlier that year she herself had been operated on for cancer of the thyroid. For twelve to fourteen years before the operation she had had an enlarged lymph node but since it had stopped growing she did not pay much attention to it. Then it changed, was diagnosed as malignant, and she had it operated on. However, four to five years before the diagnosis, she began having dreams in which something was eating away at her neck. At the time she did not know she had cancer and couldn't understand why she would dream about her neck. Evidently her unconscious was trying to alert her to something that needed attention, either on the physical or psychological level, or both. Dreams may register organic conditions occurring in the body.

Organs and parts of the body may also have symbolic meaning in dreams; that is, they may refer to the function or role played by that part or organ within the body's processes, or to the relationship by which that part connects the person to the external world.

Speaking first of the bodily function involved and what it symbolizes, we may recognize, for example, how the digestive system, in its various stages and functions, offers a whole series of processes and images which, instead of being seen for their medical significance, may be viewed as having a psychological meaning. Thus, the digestive process as a whole can be taken as a metaphor of individuation: foreign material is broken down and its nutrients absorbed so that they become integrated and transformed into the whole life of the person. Likewise, images of the digestive process may refer to the psychological process by which a new thought or understanding is "digested" and absorbed into the life of the person, thereby transforming him. Dreams of nausea or vomiting, for instance, may indicate difficulty in appropriating the new material, or images of choking or difficulty in swallowing may refer to "difficulty in swallowing (ingesting)" a new idea. Chewing, as the first stage of digestion, may refer to the process of psychotherapy or psychoanalysis or to one's own breaking down of the basic material of one's dreams and experience. Extending the metaphor, images of teeth may refer to one's ability to take hold of the stuff of life and to begin the process of transforming it into nourishment for our psychological and spiritual growth. Dentists and dental work as images in dreams may be drawing attention to the need to fix this initial function of being able to break down life material and get it ready for assimilation.

Similarly, images of elimination, toilet dreams, successful and unsuccessful, may refer to completing the cycle and cleansing the body of the by-products of the transformative process. Letting go of anger, resentment, jealousies, grudges is an essential part of the individuation process. Giving up control, pride, or fear is equally part of the elimination that is vital, if the spirit is to be well. Further mention could be made of the "filtering" metaphor of liver and kidneys, the "control" and "containment" aspects of bowels and bladder, and the "anger" aspect of the last two as well.

Toilet dreams are especially important indicators of psychological health, whether the system is working well or not. People who are highly controlled, or who hold on to their anger, harboring grudges, or are unwilling to forgive, may frequently produce dreams in which they are unable to complete a bowel movement or they may have a full toilet and be unable to flush it. Typically, the plumbing won't work, the toilet is broken, the bathroom is strewn with excrement. The embarrassment or helplessness that frequently accompany these dreams serve to underline the difficulty these people have in letting go of sensitive material. Images of stopped-up plumbing systems in my experience also may occur where there is difficulty in completing a function because of indecision, inaction or passivity.

Various organs and parts of the body similarly serve a

psychological role in enabling the person to relate to the external world. Hands and feet, and sense organs, have their obvious importance in this regard. Lungs function to draw life from the surrounding air and the process of breathing, holding onto the invisible source of life, is symbolically connected with all things of the spirit, hope and exhilaration. Sex organs are fundamentally relational, as well, and essential in establishing and maintaining the conjugal relationship.

When an image in a dream shows a part of the body as injured or swollen, one way to work on the image is to amplify the injury. In your imagination see the injury as more serious, the swelling as getting larger and larger, and see the effect that follows. The message may come when the extreme is experienced.

Those wanting to work on body symbols in dreams could use the following questions:

Body parts and organs identified?

What psychological process may be symbolized by the body image in the dream?

What relationship and message may the body image be identifying?

General Considerations

Dreams tell an unfolding story. Each individual dream is like a scene in a drama. It would be misleading, indeed impossible, to arrive at an accurate understanding of the meaning of a play on the basis of only one or two scenes. A single dream treated in isolation does not do justice to the message of the unconscious. Our dreams, therefore, need to be put in sequence and seen in relation to each other, so that the development of images and themes can be understood.

With that in mind, I am suggesting that in using the above format of dream analysis you date and keep the completed worksheets until you have several months of dreams in hand. Then review them side by side, category by category, in sequence. Some people have kept their dreams for years in dream journals and find that going back and reading over previous dreams can be quite helpful, even without the detailed analysis of a worksheet. The different tone or use of images in dreams from earlier in one's life can be striking. At the same time, the sameness of certain images or themes may stand out strongly.

You, the dreamer, are the key authority on the rightness of an association to an image in your dream. Your personal associations should be sought first before transpersonal or cultural meanings are advanced. Even when cultural or archetypal associations are made they need to "ring" or "click" with you, the same as your personal associations. Unless you have the sense of that inner truth, don't accept an interpretation as valid for you. Some of those associations that "click" may be consistent with common symbolic identifications, for example, "a dog is faithfulness" or "a dog is a spirit-guide," but often the symbols in your dreams will have their own unique associations for you as well. Usually it is not a matter of either/or; symbols may speak on different levels at the same time, and both personal and transpersonal meanings may apply.

As mentioned previously, the meaning of dreams is best accessed by participation in the story, images and symbols of our dreams. We need to experience and feel them from the inside, as it were. It is also true that sometimes the significance of a dream will become clear with just the opposite approach of detachment. It is possible to become so close to a dream that you are blind to its significance. At such times, in order to put it in perspective, you need to objectify the dream, as if you were standing back from it, or as if it were someone else's dream. This is one of the most difficult tasks in trying to work on our own dreams by ourselves. Having another person there to reflect on the dream gives that needed objectivity. Having that other person ask a question or say the same words that you have said in telling the dream, may have the effect of allowing you, the dreamer, to see your dream in a fresh way. Also, there is an added energy in the interaction between two people that greatly assists in opening up the mystery of a dream.

If you have to work alone, writing out your dreams is a good first step at objectification. A detailed worksheet with a systematic approach, such as outlined above, helps you go further. Without it, or analysis with another person, to give you objectivity, a dreamer may be so close to the dream that he may still have the assumptions of the dream ego and may miss factors that are thus skipped over.

The worksheet provided at the end of the book incorporates the program of dream analysis set out above. By analyzing dreams according to this format and accumulating the analyses side by side over time, you will be able to compare the various categories, content, images, themes, etc., across many dreams, and thus become better aware of your own unique dream language and personal symbol system. Certain themes, settings or symbols may come to have a definite significance for you, especially if they repeat in connection with similar events or circumstances in your daily life. Patterns will emerge from the accumulated dreams and connections may appear that were not evident in the individual dreams.

Here I would mention again the importance of having a backup person available when doing active imagination. Most often there is no difficulty, but it is possible to find oneself being drawn too deeply into the unconscious. The safeguards are to have a strong ego, that is, to have a sure sense of your own reality, and to have someone there with you whose presence can ground you solidly in reality.

Earlier I sounded a note of caution in regard to opening yourself up to negative influences. There is a debate about whether the shadow part of the unconscious contains evil which, if brought into consciousness, could be destructive or whether all of the shadow may safely be participated in. This is a fundamentally important question and therefore I suggested earlier that one observe one's own feelings before doing active imagination with a dangerous figure, or before confronting one's monster figures. I believe that God is the ultimate guide when it comes to these matters. As the One who stands behind all of our life and is the Lover of our souls, He can be trusted to protect us from evil and to guide us into truth and health, as we look to Him. I would, therefore, encourage those who may have doubts or fears about evil-feeling figures or images to pray for God's direction and discernment in these things. Apart from these special cases, I find prayer an indispensable help in regard to dream work generally, both in understanding dreams and in receiving dreams in answer to specific needs.

8
DREAM ANALYSIS USING WORKSHEET FORMAT: CASE DEMONSTRATIONS

In analyzing dreams using this format, not all categories or questions are usually appropriate or necessary to be used with each dream. In the following worksheet analyses of dreams, those categories that didn't apply or were not used are not recorded here.

To see how the dream analysis format described in the previous chapter looks in action, we turn now to the following demonstrations in which it is applied to three actual dreams.

Dream #1: "Border Crossing"

Ralph (not his real name), a middle-aged Canadian whose analysis was uncovering early childhood fears of rejection, had the following dream:

I am a tourist sight-seeing along the border of Canada and the United States. The Canadian side, where I am travelling, is a high cliff, like a fortification. The edge at the top is like the bottom row of teeth in a person's mouth, sharp, coming to an edge, and a bit jagged. We are trying to locate on the outer rock my position behind the wall; but the outer marking does not coincide with the inner one. It feels as if the combination would open if the inner and outer coincided.

Content

1. The setting:

The scene is a natural setting in which a high ridge of rock on the Canadian side towers over the lower rolling countryside of the U.S. The border seems to be a river which runs between the two.

2. The images:

A granite ridge forming a natural wall along the top; a few tourists standing behind the wall; someone from the U.S. side pointing out a location on the rock face, it seems, with a long pointer.

3. Main theme:

To locate the spot on the outside of the wall that matches where I stood inside.

4. The action or effect:

The whole attention is focused on finding the exact spot on the outside of the wall behind which I stood on the inside. This is not accomplished in the dream: the outer marking is still some distance from the correct position.

5. Feeling tone in the dream:

Enjoyment touring an interesting area; exhilaration, excitement centering on the quest to find the right location.

Context

6. The feeling on waking:

No noticeable difference; puzzlement.

7. *Previous day's events:*

I had had some medical tests the day before which ruled out illness, but had been uncomfortable.

8. *Emotional landscape:*

In addition to the medical examination, which had been feared, I had felt the struggle of wrestling with my fear of rejection and my need for intimacy. I anticipate the struggle to go on.

Associations

9. *What does your dream make you think of or remember?*

Of the Niagara Falls region where I travelled as a boy with my father.

12. *What similarities does this dream have to other dreams you've had?*

I can recall dreams over several years in which I was on the border between Canada and the U.S. For all of those years I had entertained the hope of being able to relocate my business in the U.S. In one vivid dream, I was in the U.S. walking south toward the edge of a high plateau. I knew that beyond that edge lay the "promised land." As I reached it, I was surprised to find a great river at the bottom of the hill and across the river stretched rolling fields of garden-like beauty.

Amplification

15. *How are you like the persons, animals, objects in the dream?*

I realize that I have a structure in me like the granite

ridge, a defensiveness or division between my inner and outer selves. I need to hide behind a wall at times to keep my inner world private and safe. At the same time, I identify with those who are trying to point out the correct spot on the outer wall. This seems like the analysis I am involved in, in which my analyst and I are trying to bring the outer and inner worlds together.

20. Completion: If the dream is incomplete, what ending would you give to it?

At first, I thought I would like to have those on the outside find the place that corresponded to the inner position I had occupied. It would be like the last turn of a combination lock and with the two marks coming together there would be an opening. But as I think of that happening I become aware of anxiety: such an opening would give "them" access and I would be vulnerable. I feel more comfortable if the search is prolonged for a while and the outer probing still is off the mark.

22. New knowledge: What does this dream tell you about yourself and others that you did not know before?

I knew about the wall within myself before and how a part of me has withdrawn and hidden for protection. What is new is the explicit focus on the attempt to bring the outer and inner worlds together. I could actually feel the openness that would take place if they were to coincide and I had a painful response to being vulnerable in that open position. The other new, yet old, factor was that only by the defensiveness being unlocked, the vulnerability risked, could I ever hope to enter the "promised land."

23. *Conscious response: What question, action, or decision do you want to make in response to this dream?*

The dream showed me how I cling to my hiddenness and fear exposure. At the same time I want to find the combination that would unlock me from inhibitions and fears. It makes me wonder if the U.S. in the dream might stand for "us," the world of togetherness with others. The decision that came out of working on the dream was to press on with the task of bringing the inner and the outer to an opening.

Comment: This is the dream of a man who had been in analysis for several years and was knowledgeable about depth psychology. His responses reflect his long practice of studying his dreams for self-awareness. The time sequence does not show in the above record, but the responses, recorded above, contain associations and insights that continued to come to light even a month or more after his initial working on the dream. Remembering the pointer (#2), for example, which was not in the original recollection of the dream, and associating the U.S. with "us" and the world of togetherness with others (#23), were later awarenesses. There was also a shift, recorded in #20, from his first eagerness to bring the outer and inner points together and make an opening, to his later awareness of anxious reluctance to have the inner come open too soon. This unfolding of the dream into ever larger significance and increasingly subtle distinctions shows how dreams continue to grow in enlightening consciousness.

The dream came at an important point, well-advanced in his analysis, when he was exploring his early experiences of alienation, abandonment and invasion which had set him in a defensive stance toward others. A key memory was of a series of enemas administered in the first weeks of his life by a threatening nurse figure. In adulthood, when not playing safe and rewarding roles, his typical posture was to withdraw emotionally, and to endure isolation rather than risk the terrifying possibility of either rejection or invasion of his inner space. This background may help us understand some of the images and symbols of the dream and how he understood their meaning.

Dream #2: "Forbidden fruit"

Cynthia, whose lengthy first marriage had ended in divorce and who had recently embarked on her second marriage, had the following dream.

My husband and I are walking along a country road. We see a beautiful apple tree in a field behind a chain-link fence. The apples are perfect and beautiful and there are a lot of them. Two other people who are walking along climb easily over the fence, get two apples and walk off, eating them. My husband climbs over the fence and gets me one. But we see the farmer and his wife walking over, and I say, "Oh, now we're in trouble," but we don't run— we wait for them. They don't scold us, but say that because of their nearness to the city, the apples are poisoned by _____ (a long chemical name which I know is made up), so I laugh and peel the apple with my teeth and go on eating it. It is delicious.

Then as we walk along we see a young woman (I seem to feel it is my husband's ex-wife). She climbs over a fence and onto the back of a bull, which is in a chute and I think she's showing off. She's safe because the bull is in a chute. But it opens and the animal charges out; somehow it has become a chestnut stallion. I'm a little concerned for her. She falls off and two men come out to grab the horse; but I realize the horse is gentle and it just sniffs at her as she lies on the ground.

We continue on, walking to our car, and I see a long train going by slowly. Flat-cars come along with life-size models of horses in a prancing position. There are four, each a different color and on its own flat-bed. I think to myself: that store is sending its Christmas decorations for storage. Sure enough, more cars come by with beautiful sleighs on them. Then I see four trunks with rounded tops and watch as they slide off the train right in front of me. On each trunk is a quilt in pastel colors and I see people coming along. A girl says, "Oh, this one is pretty" and takes it. I look at one and think how nice it would be on (my grandson's) bed. I go to pick it up and my husband says "You can't do that; it doesn't belong to you." I say ruefully, "Yes, I know. It's too bad it's so pretty and I know the others will take it." I leave it and get into the car.

1. The Setting:

Rural, flat country, fields.

2. The Images:

Fences, chain-link fences marking off fields, dirt roads, only tree is the (perfect) apple tree; husband of dreamer, two other people (men?), farmer and wife; big, beautiful apples. Bull in a chute; stallion; young woman; two men. Car, train, flat-cars; four life-size model horses; sleighs; four trunks; four quilts; people; girl.

3. The Main Theme:

Having something wonderful that people try to tell me is wrong (poison) for me; but I know that they are wrong.

4. The Action or Effect:

Seeing the apple, how beautiful it is, how delicious. Pleasure at eating it. Knowing they've made up the long name as an excuse just to stop us from eating the apples and they are wrong. Being told that something attractive can't be had because it belongs to someone else.

5. The Feeling Tone in the Dream:

Laughing, happy, pleasure; some passing concern, mild regret.

Context

6. The Feeling on Waking:

Mild pleasure, interest.

7. Previous Day's Events:

Marriage of husband's son where his ex-wife and family are present.

8. Emotional Landscape: What emotional focus was there the day before the dream?

Strange sort of detachment; not feeling part of things— a bystander. Disappointment over family insensitivity.

Associations

9. What associations do you have to any of the images in the dream?

It's nice to be in the country. I used to live in the

country. Apples=something forbidden; bull=mortal danger from goring; behind fences=belonging to someone else; former husband=a "bull in a china shop;" stallion=not as dangerous; horses, sleighs, trunks=things we used to have in first marriage; old things. Quilts=heirlooms, old possessions; pastels=colors I wouldn't pick, baby colors for grandson.

10. *What in your life has been similar to elements in the dream?*

That things pass me by, like the train. All these things (of a lifetime) are in passing (tears).

That things are not what they seem to be: the beautiful apples, it seems you shouldn't have them; the cars have landed the trunks, quilts, right in front of you, but you can't have them; the bull turns into a stallion.

Amplification

13. *Balance: b. What conscious attitude might this dream be trying to balance or compensate?*

My concern over my husband, the church and others saying that remarriage is wrong.

c. *What does it add to your usual way of living or thinking?*

It confirms that I don't accept the teaching about divorce and remarriage being wrong.

14. *Active Imagination (Go back into the dream and dialogue with the people, animals, objects.): What came out of the dialogue?*

With Farmer: "I don't want people to get the apples;

but I don't want to get after them; so we made up the story of the poison." (Why doesn't husband eat an apple?) "He doesn't want one."

Train: "I'm taking these things a long way away." (Why did the trunks fall off?) "Because you might like to have them." (But husband said that would be like taking somebody else's.) Train said, "Too bad you missed out."

15. Gestalt: How are you like the persons, animals, objects in the dream?

I'm like the woman who got on the bull to show off.

18. What question might this dream be answering?

Is it wrong to remarry after divorce?

20. Completion: If the dream is disturbing to you, what would bring resolution?

If the apples could be eaten without anyone finding fault, and the quilt could be taken without any guilt.

22. New Knowledge: What does this dream tell you about yourself and others that you did not know before?

Helps to balance the idea that it's wrong to remarry after divorce.

23. Conscious Response: What question, action, or decision do you want to make in response to this dream?

I want to be affirmed in what I think and not let other people put their opinions and judgments on me about remarriage. This confirms that my life is in chapters and that when a chapter is finished I go on to the next chapter. My previous life is complete and I am going on in this marriage.

Comment: Such a full dream with so many rich images and in three parts like this calls for a more detailed analysis than is possible here. Let me touch only on some highlights.

The apple tree symbol summons up the Genesis story of Adam's seduction by Eve and identifies the theme of desire and sexual temptation. Cynthia associates the apple with "something forbidden," yet the dream does not condemn them for taking one, and two others (indicating considerable psychic energy) have done the same thing. Rather, the emphasis is put, first, on the difficulties of maintaining the rules of ownership (marriage): the apples belong to the farm couple who make up a frightening story in order to keep their apples (when the fences aren't respected), a story which doesn't work; and, second, the emphasis is on the pleasure of fulfilling desire: Cynthia eats the apple without remorse and enjoys it immensely. Although she acknowledges the rules of ownership and in her dream ego (which is closest to her conscious attitude) feels some guilt when caught, the dream attitude generally is one of permission and taking advantage of rather lax enforcement of the rules.

This same attitude of "laissez-faire" is expressed in the third section of the dream when she wants to take a quilt that has become available in the train wreck. Her active imagination tells her that even the train laments her missing the opportunity. It is her husband who sounds the prohibition and enforces an ownership that is by no means clear. Interestingly, in the first section her husband had not eaten an apple. She indicated that, in fact, her husband is more troubled by remarriage than she, which suggests that the husband figure in the dream, rather than being interpreted as an animus figure, should be taken objectively as her actual husband.

The young woman in the second part of the dream was seen either as her husband's ex-wife or as a shadow figure of herself. As Cynthia came to associate the bull with her first husband, she could accept the validity that this female figure was also a part of herself. During the early stages of her marriage (when the bull was still in the chute=committed to the marriage?) she had felt safe and protected by him; but with his acting out sexually (the chute opens and the bull transforms into the chestnut stallion?) she gave up on the marriage. In view of the fact that this dream followed a family wedding in which she met her husband's ex-wife, it is likely commenting on both her husband's ex-wife (which was her first identification) and herself, with the regard to a struggle they both have: how to manage the strong life force of sexuality which can turn from being nurturing and protective within a committed relationship to being dangerous when the commitment is broken. This could be both in reference to their husbands' sexuality and their own. The gentle sniffing of the stallion would tend to be reassuring and to calm those fears.

The third section seems like a slow parade of her life. She has sad feelings and tears, sensing that all these things are "in passing." The repeated fours—horses, trunks, quilts—indicate completion of all that is old, heritage. The two things that lie ahead with interest are a quilt (for a grandson?) and getting in the car with her husband (getting on with their life together?).

The dream appears to confirm the rightness of her desire for her second marriage, in spite of some contrary opinions about remarriage, and appears to offer a review of her past life and letting go of it.

Although Cynthia did not comment on any archetypal elements, it is possible to detect that dimension at a number points in the dream. The train sliding the trunks and quilts off right in front of Cynthia expresses a fortuitous synchronicity or "coincidence" which is further enhanced by the comment in active imagination giving permission to take a quilt. This coming off the tracks (train tracks often indicate collective rigidity and undeviating conformity) so conveniently suggests a *deus ex machina* behind the scenes, favoring her. In the first section, the farmer and wife have an archetypal sense of the divine gardener who is non-confrontative, non-judgmental. The bull symbol calls up the archetypal bull found, for example, in Mithraism (an ancient Greek religion) where it stands for the primary life force. In view of Cynthia's personal association of the bull with the safety she felt with her first husband, the question arises as to what degree she may be unaware of the more potent possibilities of the bull (her first husband?) hurting her. If the meaning is restricted to the association she makes consciously (although her ex-husband is like a bull in a china shop she felt protected by him in the early stages of their marriage), the transformation of the bull into the stallion in the dream suggests a shift from the protective mother complex (bull, though masculine, is still bovine) to the sexual.

Dream #3: Grass and Sand

Isabelle is a married woman who, in spite of an unhappy marriage and occasional fantasies about other men, has remained in her marriage.

I am at home in my back yard looking over the fence and see my neighbor who is caring for his garden. He is a fine gardener and it shows in his beautiful green grass and shrubs. As I watch a sandstorm comes up. The grass fades and becomes sand. Everything in his yard becomes brown and sandy. The sandstorm is terrible. I feel it sting my face. I think, "I'd rather have a snowstorm than a sandstorm."

1. The Setting:

Suburban back yards, my own and my neighbor's.

2. The Images:

Flower beds, trees and paths in my yard; wooden fence; man next door, green grass, pruned shrubs.

3. The Main Theme:

Beautiful green garden becomes brown and dry in sandstorm.

4. The Action or Effect:

In a sudden sandstorm the lush green life in my neighbor's yard fades and dries up, leaving a sandy desert. The sand hurts my face and leaves me wishing it had been a snowstorm instead.

5. The Feeling Tone in the Dream:

Interest and appreciation followed by sadness and dismay.

Context

6. The Feeling on Waking:

Puzzled.

7. Previous Day's Events:

Nothing special, routine.

8. Emotional Landscape: a. What emotional focus was there the day before the dream?

Usual marital coldness, barbed comments, withdrawal by husband.

Associations

9. What associations do you have to any of the images in the dream?

sand=dry, no life, gritty
sandstorm=desert, nomads, camels, eyes shut waiting out storm
green grass=plenty, alive, growing
fence=wooden, high
neighbor=at one time I liked him, fantasized about him

10. What in your life has been similar to elements in the dream?

I have times of enthusiasm, big plans, and hopes that suddenly fade and I feel disappointed. My relation with my husband is stormy and cold like a snowstorm.

12. What similarities does this dream have to other dreams you've had?

I've never dreamed of sandstorms before. I've had some dreams of other men who attracted me, but not many.

Amplification

13. Balance: c. What does it add to your usual way of living or thinking?

There is a shock value in the sudden storm and the dramatic change from lush green garden to sandstorm and everything sandy, as if something is trying to get my attention or make a point.

21. Archetypal Identity: What evidence is there of the presence of transpersonal or archetypal connection in the dream?

The wind suggests the divine spirit is moving in the transformation that is taking place. It is powerful, sudden and mysterious, and its force driving the sand is so strong it hurts.

Puns: I considered the possibility of a pun quite by accident. As I focus on the fence which separates the two back yards, ours so drab and his so green, suddenly I realize "the grass is greener on the other side of the fence." Sometimes in the past I had compared him with my husband and thought how I would have preferred him.

22. New Knowledge: What does this dream tell you about yourself and others that you did not know before?

Once I made the connection of comparing my husband to the man next door ("the grass is greener on the other side of the fence"), I realized that the dream was telling me that my attraction to the neighbor had changed. I no longer looked at him with desire; that had somehow dried up. I also realized that, although my husband was cold and unloving toward me (snowstorm), I now preferred him to the neighbor.

23. Conscious Response: What question, action, or decision do you want to make in response to this dream?

The dream surprised me by showing me how my feelings had changed toward the man next door and also, by comparison, toward my husband. As a result, I feel a bit more content to work on our marriage.

Comment: The dream with its remarkable storm that turns things upside down is similar to the magical transformations in fairy tales. Such events reflect the archetypal action of the collective unconscious and indicate important stages in individuation. In Isabelle's case, we can see a projection being pulled back from the neighbor who was an object of her fantasies and a more realistic attitude emerging toward her husband.

This ends the case demonstrations using the worksheet format to analyze dreams. More detailed examples of the use of this format will be found in chapter 11 where the practical value of such dream analysis will be discussed.

Understanding How Dreams Can Be Helpful

9
WHAT DO THE SYMBOLS IN DREAMS REPRESENT?

We turn now to the practical question of how to make use of the material that has been brought out by the dream analysis format developed in the last chapter. Having considered the content of a dream with its images and symbols, looked at the context and found connections to your daily life, made associations to the various dream images, and amplified them as best you can, what then? Some images in our dreams are of people, places or objects known to us and the meaning might be obvious in the light of some life situation in which we were involved with that person or object in the previous day or so. This is the objective understanding of a dream, where the dream is communicating something about that actual person or object or about our relationship with them. Many dreams, however, are about images and persons that we do not recognize and the meaning is by no means clear. They contain images of anonymous people and of objects and places that are more general than specific and seem to relate more to our inner than our outer life.

Two Types of Dreams
There appear, therefore, to be two basic types of dreams: dreams based on the processing of daily experience in the light of our personal memory, body-

123

medical state and creative problem solving; and dreams
that reflect the deep structures of our mind and that
express the forms of human thought itself. For those who
might want to explore this further, Harry Hunt has
described these two types and developed a model
understanding of dreaming in his book, *The Multiplicity
of Dreams*.

The first kind of dream is concerned with reorganizing
and integrating our personal memory in the light of the
day's events, a kind of practical problem-solving focus
that could be readily understood in terms of what Freud
called the "day residue." Such dreams might have fairly
obvious personal meaning and need little interpretation.
Simply recounting this kind of dream to yourself or
writing it down to make it clearer will often be all that is
needed to reveal its meaning.

What Hunt calls the "archetypal" kind of dream,
however, depends on factors more removed from day-to-
day events and brings us in touch with the deep
structures of human thought that seek to produce an
overall integration of individual life. This kind of dream is
highly imaginative and depends on an ability to
appreciate symbols. It is to this second kind of dream, the
dream that requires the interpretation of symbols, that we
turn our attention now. What is revealed through the
symbols in these dreams?

Jung's Model of the Psyche

To answer that question we need to probe further into
the model of the psyche developed by Carl Jung which we
introduced in chapter 3. According to this explanation,
the symbols in dreams represent aspects of ourselves
which are hidden in the unconscious. Earlier we spoke of
the individual's consciousness being like an island and the
unconscious being like the underwater foundation which

goes down to bedrock. Beneath the island of consciousness lie the hidden depths of the personal unconscious,
containing the genetic heritage and socializing factors,
now largely forgotten, that have shaped that unique
individual and belong to that person alone. Under the
personal unconscious are levels of what Jung called the
"collective unconscious," which holds the shared
experience of the whole human race as well as
fundamental realities that have never been known.
Together, these two levels of the unconscious contain the
person's resources both of his own individuality and also
of the collective mind shared by all humanity.

In order to describe what unconscious material dream
symbols express, it is necessary to introduce a concept
that is difficult to grasp or to explain. It is the concept of
"archetypes."

Archetypes

What we find when we study the material brought up
by dreams is that it reflects the full range of human
experience, both personal or collective. In dreams we
may be terrified by a fierce animal, excited by a lover,
enchanted by the beauty of a mountain lake. These, and
other dream images, reflect experiences which have
been embedded in either our personal or collective
unconscious. Deep within us, attitudes, values, viewpoints, have taken shape through the impact of life
experience. It is as though "little personalities" have
formed according to the hurts, stresses or encourage-
ments of life. These mini-identities respond to the events
of our day-to-day life by acting themselves out in the
images in our dreams. Jung called these inner characters,
or little personalities, which have been formed through
the individual's own life experience, "complexes." We
shall return to describe them later in this chapter. Deeper

than the complexes, are basic life patterns which have been formed through the compound experience of humanity through the ages. These basic patterns, which provide a kind of foundational structure for life, Jung called "archetypes."

In trying to understand what dreams reveal, it may help to think of the unconscious being like a great theater with a cast of thousands and a prop room filled with images. These are the various "people" and images that inhabit our dreams. But they follow scripts and act out their parts according to something deeper and unseen. These guiding principles, "blueprints" or patterns of life, which are reflected in the images of our dreams, are the "archetypes."

Archetypes are "universal patterns of human experience" present in the collective unconscious of humanity. In every person, for example, there is a basic sense of what a mother is. Behind all of the varied images of mothers and mothering influences in people's dreams, there is a "mother" archetype, a basic pattern of motherness that contains all of these. The actual dream image which a certain dreamer experiences is not itself the archetype, but a reflection of it. The archetype is an abstract idea or pattern on which the individual dream image is modelled. It is abstract because an archetype itself never becomes conscious. It may only be known through images of it becoming conscious. "When the image becomes conscious it takes on content and is then filled out with the material of conscious experience" (Jung). So, when we dream, it is a specific kind of mother of which we dream; the archetype is only known through the image which is clothed with conscious content, that is, it becomes limited to a specific kind of mother. The pattern of "motherness" has found expression in your dream as this mother who is radiant and smiling, or that mother who is judgmental and stern, and so on.

Similarly, there are archetypes that correspond to the basic patterns of all our human experience. We have a basic pattern for father, king, queen, clown, healer, and so on. We have reason to believe that the collective unconscious contains the distilled experience of the human race and is a storehouse of humanity's wisdom. So all of the patterns of universal experience may be said to be present there, from snakes to medicine men. Our dreams reveal certain basic patterns that provide structure to the wealth of human experience as it is caught in the deep unconscious. The archetypes are more, however, than the sum of human experience, as if they were just the accumulated deposits of human living: they are more primary than human life and provide "blueprints" by which life experience itself may be interpreted.

Four Basic Archetypes

The nature of archetypes will become clearer when we look at the four basic archetypes of which Jung speaks. They are the "persona," the "anima-animus," the "shadow," and the "Self." Strictly speaking, the ego is also an archetype in Jung's understanding. Unlike the other archetypes, it is conscious. The closest the unconscious comes to the ego in dreams is when the dreamer experiences himself in a dream. This "dream-ego" represents an attitude closest to the conscious attitude.

Self

Most people have the sense that dreams are "given," that is, that they are not of our conscious creation. There is a sense of some "other" who is involved in devising or crafting our dreams—a mind at work behind the images and stories. In terms of the theater metaphor, there is some mind or purpose behind the script and the whole production, a director. This "other" Jung called the Self.

The Self is what Jung called the divine archetype. It is "the unifying and ordering center of the total psyche (both conscious and unconscious), the seat of objective reality." As such, it is the central organizing principle over all. Whereas the ego is the center of consciousness, that is, where each person comes to a focus of awareness in the individual "I," the Self as the center of the whole personality is unknown and unknowable. There is, however, a dialogue between the Self and the ego which is carried on through dreams. We may think of the images in dreams, then, as bridges connecting the Self in our inner depths with our focused consciousness, the ego. Dream images carry up into consciousness what is hidden in the unconscious structures of the archetypes and organized by the Self.

Typically, the Self is represented by religious figures, a wonderful child, or a mandala (round) wholeness image such as the sun, the globe or a clock face. The Madonna and Child, Jesus, Moses or Buddha, according to your religious tradition, may all be images of the Self. Because the Self is so central to the psyche and invested with energy, it presents itself in images that often have a sense of what Jung called "the numinous," inspiring awe in those who behold it.

Figures of quaternity, as in a square or a squared circle, may also represent the wholeness of the Self. Fourness, two pairs in balance, has the sense of stability and completion to a stage of development. When rotated, a quaternary symbol becomes a circle, which is a frequent symbol of the Self.

I once had a dream in which I was leading a group in

prayer in a church basement. The people were seated in rows with a few at the end perpendicular to the others. As I prayed, a large orange which I held in my hand unpeeled spontaneously as I turned it, as if by an unseen knife. When I finished the prayer, the winding strip of orange peel that I had cut, came off the top of the orange like a cap. Inside was empty. Suddenly, the orange became a globe of the world. In the process, the spherical frame of the globe was revealed. What looked like coat-hanger wire formed the longitudinal lines and corresponded to the divisions between what would have been sections of the orange. Although there were people involved in the dream and some ecstatic response on their part, the most significant factors in the dream seemed to be this unusual display of unseen power and the parallel rows of seats on which the people were seated. It suggested to me a contrast between the spherical globe and the parallel rows of seats, between the supernatural power of prayer and the formal lining-up of the people. The way the dream put those together seemed to indicate an unfolding and infiltration of that unlimited power into the set lines of institutional religion. The symbol of the globe often represents the Self. The numinous sense of wonder which came with its effortless action was the highlight of the dream for me.

Earlier we said that the ego may be defined as the center of consciousness. Jung sees the Self as the center of the whole psyche, both conscious and unconscious. This may be schematized as shown on page 130.

The Self, as the organizing principle of the individual psyche, is commonly understood to be the giver of dreams.

Persona

The persona expresses the various ways in which the person relates to the outside world. Jung defined the

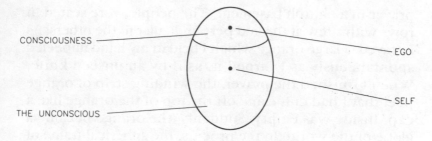

CONSCIOUSNESS

EGO

SELF

THE UNCONSCIOUS

INDIVIDUAL PSYCHE

FIGURE 3

persona as "the individual's system of adaptation to, or the manner he assumes in dealing with, the world." It refers to the roles we play or masks we wear and, in dreams, may be seen in images of work function, professional identity or personal relationship. Common persona figures might cast the dreamer in the role of nurse or doctor, teacher, mother, father, or foreman, for example.

Some years ago, Irving Goffman wrote a book entitled *The Presentation of Self in Everyday Life*, which beautifully describes how we behave in certain ways according to the social expectations of a position or job. He asks us to imagine the waiters in a fashionable dining room, elegantly dressed and waiting on tables with decorum. However, passing through the swinging door into the kitchen, their demeanor alters drastically. Instantly, they relax into another mode of being, laughing, joking, talking slang or slouching and taking a furtive drag on a cigarette. Once back through the swinging door, they become models of propriety again as they move back into their "waiter" persona.

An individual may have several "personas," being son, husband, father, brother, perhaps, and machinist, baseball coach and lodge member. In each of these, he would exhibit different aspects of his personality. How he would act in one setting might not suit in another setting. Being able to move effortlessly from one persona role to another is an accomplishment and indicates a richness of personality.

In that the persona represents the various roles we play, it may also be expressed in images of clothing. A person may dream, for example, of preparing to take a shower, but first having to strip off layer upon layer of clothing. The clothing is like a kind of protection, a way of presenting yourself in the world without showing your core being. The more external the clothing, the more distant that role might be from showing the intimate inner person. So, being bundled up in a heavy overcoat might indicate a need to play a role that insulates one from the cold winds of criticism. In contrast, dreams of being in one's underwear might indicate a very revealing role where one is willing to be vulnerable or just feels vulnerable. Nakedness might express an absence of any role playing, a position in which the true ego is open to being seen as it is, a state of intimacy.

Of the various archetypes, personas come closest to the border with consciousness and we are often aware of playing persona roles. However, the way we play a role is governed largely by unconscious factors. Sometimes a person is so identified with a role that he is not conscious of being anything other than that role. In our culture, physicians, professors, and clergy are personas which call for great dedication and commitment, and lend themselves to becoming so overwhelming that the non-professional life of the person is crowded out and the person may become identified with that role alone. In that case, he is living out an unconscious identity. Such automatic living is governed by habit and indicates little or no development of individuality or uniqueness. The person is a servant to the role, rather than the role serving the person's wishes or needs.

Animus-anima

Another basic pattern that structures the psyche is that of sexual identity and attraction. This archetype is the anima or animus, from the Latin "mind" or "spirit." The animus-anima refers to the contra-sexual figure in dreams that may relate positively or negatively to our conscious ego. It may function in dreams as an expression of the largely unconscious feminine aspect of a man (anima) or the largely unconscious masculine aspect of a woman (animus).

It is important to note that the animus-anima concept is not about sexual gender but about psychological qualities. The animus is masculine, not male; the anima is feminine, not female. Typically, the masculine principle embodies goal-striving, achievement, like an arrow that flies to the target without feeling or concern for how it gets there; the feminine principle, in contrast, is more relational, taken up with feeling and valuing the context of being.

In a man's dream, when it is positive, the anima might appear as the woman of his dreams. A good example is found in a dream I had some ten years ago. In my dream I encountered "my" woman who invited me to come with her to help her pick out a dress. She said she wanted me to be with her because I had such good taste and she loved me. We went to a dress shop where my elegant woman tried on a marvellous scarlet and white dress. It was designed of long thin triangles of satin cloth that hung at various lengths from her shoulders. With a bank of mirrors behind her, she twirled on a raised platform in front of me to show it off. Long afterward, I can still see that sight of her twirling before me, the dress's red and white pleats swishing, and her lovely legs and ankles showing beneath for my delight. What is more, I can still sense the warmth and excitement of her presence within me. Here was an aspect of my anima.

Many students of Jungian psychology think that the animus-anima is the archetype which relates the person to the collective unconscious. It is a bridge to the man's soul or the woman's spirit.

Shadow

Images that express values or life-style contrary to the conscious position of the person indicate the shadow archetype. The shadow is the inferior part of the personality, the "sum of all personal and collective psychic elements which, because of their incompatibility with the chosen conscious attitude, are denied expression in life...a 'splinter personality' with contrary tendencies in the unconscious"(Jung). It is a same-sex figure as the dreamer but represents something opposite to the dreamer's conscious identity. It may express what the dreamer might become, if he or she could stretch enough to incorporate it. In that sense, it offers the dreamer a potentiality for growth and fuller, more balanced personality.

A good example is found in the following dream of a middle-aged school teacher, a married woman and mother, who had a fairly puritan view of herself. She dreamed that she was in Madrid, Spain, on a hot summer's night and, much to her dismay, found herself in the red-light district. Before her eyes, she saw a prostitute step out of a doorway into the crowded street. She was wearing only a light shift dress and sandals and, as she made her way sensuously up the narrow street, men leered after her. The dreamer even knew the woman's name—Juanita. In working on the dream, she was horrified to think that the various persons in one's dreams could be parts of oneself. Surely there could be nothing like that in her personality! But two weeks later she acknowledged that indeed there was a part of her that was more sexy than she had consciously recognized and that she had been unfair to herself and her husband in their sexual relationship. "Juanita" clearly was a part of herself, her shadow, which she had repressed.

The shadow is the dark side of the person, the part that is usually hidden from consciousness and from others. But it is not necessarily bad or evil, just opposite to the conscious ego personality. A person whose conscious identity is very worldly or criminal might have spiritual or saintly shadow figures.

Although it helps to organize our interpretation of dreams by thinking of dream images in terms of identifiable archetypes such as animus-anima, persona, shadow and Self, there is a danger that we may limit our dream work just to thinking. Merely to identify the archetype or complex is to leave things on an intellectual level and to miss the feeling value which is in the image. We need to encounter the personality in the persons and images of our dreams and experience their energy. I will have more to saw about this in the next chapter.

Complexes

Complexes arise from the personal part of the unconscious. We see from dreams that there are certain clusters of images or themes which refer to that individual alone. These may be familiar places in a person's life, such as a childhood home or a place of work, a powerful experience, such as a scene of terror or of humiliation, or a set of similar images which recur for that person. They may also be images of a familiar person such as one's parents, or of a class of person, such as an authority figure.

When these images have a particularly strong effect or persist by recurring in a person's dreams, we call them "complexes." These images reflect the particular ways our own life has unfolded. They embody the distortions and hang-ups learned in life experience. Complexes are the monuments to the battles fought in relation to persons and situations we encountered in life. From birth on, we engage in a struggle of reaching out to a strange world and facing acceptance or rejection. Each rejection challenges us to withdraw and retreat into safety. It is painful and frightening to be rejected and makes a deep impression on the personality of the young person. When enough rejections come in a particular framework or with regard to a particular person, the memories of those hurts and failures become associated in a common bundle which we call a "complex."

What is meant by a complex can be illustrated in terms of a medical condition. Early in my life I tested positive for T.B. On the chest x-ray, the doctor pointed out a cluster of small white dots, like b.b. shot or tiny grapes, in the center of my chest. "You have had T.B.," he said, "but it is not active now. Those dots are calcifications which your body produced to enclose the active bacilli so they wouldn't harm you." In a way similar to the calcifications, complexes are psychological structures which contain the hurtful experiences of our developing years. When a child has repeated experiences of pain or fear in regard to a certain situation, person or place, the energy of those negative experiences becomes associated around that situation, person or place, to form a kind of bundle of negative energy. The actual memories of those hurtful encounters may become forgotten and the bundle buried in the unconscious as a complex, but, unlike the calcification, the complex has a field of influence and casts its spell over our conscious life in the form of attitudes, moods and phobias.

Jung defines complexes as "psychic fragments which have been split off owing to traumatic influences or certain incompatible tendencies." He was describing a process by which a conscious experience went unconscious as a means of coping with something that was too much for the conscious personality to accommodate at the time. It was Jung who first coined the term "inferiority complex," referring to those experiences of inferiority which became associated in our experience. Similarly, there are "mother complexes," "father complexes," and complexes that associate to fears such as claustrophobia, the fear of closed spaces, or agoraphobia, the fear of public places. Other complexes may relate to the exercise of undue power or authority or to the presence of an obsession.

Not all complexes are negative. Some have been formed around positive experiences that for some reason were isolated or forbidden. A person may have a "power complex" in which he becomes carried away with his own authority and is used to getting his own way. Children may have repeated moments of idyllic experience with a parent which became idealized so that a positive mother or father complex formed. The effect of such a complex might be to make the person expect too much and always be dissatisfied with actual love relationships. At the heart of a complex, then, is an attitude, either positive or negative, that has become exaggerated and assumed too much importance for the well-being of the whole personality.

Complexes have a personality of their own and exert a

power which pulls and distorts normal conscious functioning whenever a person approaches a situation similar to that which originally produced the complex. A person who has some claustrophic fears, for example, may find that her whole personality is altered whenever the possibility of being confined in a small space presents itself. Her composure is shattered, her concentration gone; her palms may become sweaty, her breathing shallow, her heart races. Often the influence of a complex may be consciously felt without the person quite knowing what is at work. Mood swings and depression are typical manifestations of complexes. An office worker may wonder why the days her boss was away at a convention went so well. It might be her unconscious attitude toward authority that makes her tense when he is on the scene. A husband may be thrown into a "mood" when his wife finds fault in a voice similar to his mother's.

In dreams, complexes come out in images that express the essence of the original struggle. A common motif in the dreams of one man, for instance, was the image of being shot at. This might occur in the course of military exercises, with tanks racing across a field toward him, or soldiers with rifles coming after him. In other dreams, he would be attacked by sinister figures and criminals. Often he would dream of being a fugitive, running and hiding from those who were hunting him down with dogs and guns. In his early life, he had been raised with harsh parental discipline. Threats of punishment and rejection formed part of the discipline. He was especially sensitive to criticism. Clearly, there was a connection between the early experience and the dream images. He had internalized the threatening words and actions and turned them on himself. In adulthood, they still lived within him, but now in the form of a persecution complex.

In this example, the complex was expressed both by objects—guns, rifles, tanks, criminals—and by action being taken against him. Sometimes complexes are expressed only by objects. Images of box-cars or cargo ships, for example, with their womb-like shape, may suggest the nurturing aspect of a mother complex, as do images of milk or cows. Depending on the role it plays in the dream, such an image could refer to the tendency of the dreamer to be overly giving in his own life or possibly of being in reaction against being taken care of. Images of public buildings, such as institutional, governmental or business buildings, malls and apartment buildings, inasmuch as they are impersonal, may refer to being trapped in collective thinking, where the individual is submerged by the institution. Inasmuch as they are man-made, they may refer to structures of a person's own life experience that have been socially imposed. We could call these power or authority complexes. In contrast, the image of a house, especially one's own, or one's car, often represents one's individual life or one's body. Natural images, such as an outdoor scene, a garden, field or meadow, for example, may refer to the part of you that is free of complexes.

Similar to the way in which public buildings may represent impersonal, collective forces, railroad and subway tracks often stand for routinized thinking and having to "go along with the crowd." There is no freedom to deviate from the established way, as would be possible if you were driving your own car. The tracks might symbolize a complex of conformity and dependence. To appreciate the bound-up nature of a complex, we have only to compare the feeling associated with riding in a train on tracks with that of driving a sports car, or, even closer to our true nature, of riding a bicycle or sailing a sailboat.

Some complexes are expressed in dreams by a particular shape or configuration that presents a difficulty to the person. Being in a maze, may represent such a bind. Ralph's dream, in chapter 8, of getting the inner and outer to coincide, provides a further example of a complex. Complexes are very helpful, then, in depicting a field chart of the personal struggles and indicating unique features of the personality structure of the individual. They lay out what issues trouble the person and where she needs help. This is important, because most of the time a person does not know what her confusion is about, nor the source of her fears, obsessions and moods.

The question is often asked: What is the meaning of this symbol or that? It is tempting to assign a definite meaning to a symbol. But a symbol may have many meanings, depending on many factors, such as the context in which it is put and the dreamer's associations. As I have shown earlier, symbols speak on different levels of meaning at the same time. It is irresponsible, therefore, to equate a symbol with one meaning alone. Far better to explore the meaning or meanings it has to the dreamer and then to investigate the various meanings it has in the culture. For this purpose, a dictionary of symbols is helpful. Good symbol dictionaries give multiple meanings gleaned from literature, mythology, religion, and fairy tales. De Vries' *Dictionary of Symbols and Imagery* is almost exhaustive in its references, while Cirlot's *A Dictionary of Symbols* is less detailed, but frustrating at times by what it omits.

The *Complete Works of C. G. Jung* provides an invaluable resource of symbolism. By using the Index in each volume and especially the General Index in Volume XX, a person is able to look up Jung's treatment of a large number of individual symbols which are listed there individually or under "dreams" and "symbols." In this way the complexity of a symbol is explained and interpreted in its richness, often at length, and frequently in the dreamer's context. The writings of other analysts often explore the various meanings of symbols in actual dreams and in the context of the person's life and may be used in a similar way. Marion Woodman, for example, has written powerfully of transformation struggles in women's individuation and her works are especially rich with the symbolism of women's dreams. Another analyst, James Hall, in his *Jungian Dream Interpretation* has a short chapter on "Common Dream Motifs" as well as many references to various symbols throughout this helpful book. Again, it must be mentioned that there are no set meanings for dream symbols. Their meaning is always in relation to the dreamer and in the context of that person's life.

Another work which I have found helpful is Jeffrey's *A Dictionary of Biblical Tradition in English Literature*. Much of the meaning of our culture has been formed under religious auspices. Many images in folklore, literature, and popular language owe much of their root meaning to their birth in religious settings. The mental and emotional life of Western people cannot be explained without reference to biblical stories and symbols. This particular work offers detailed references to certain central images and concepts.

10
HOW DO DREAMS WORK FOR PERSONAL TRANSFORMATION?

It's quite possible to have a dream, to do a full analysis of its features and images and be no further ahead in your life. For example, a man had a dream in which he was visiting an impressive office building, but behind the scenes he saw workmen trying to build foundation walls and meeting with disaster after disaster. In trying to understand his dream, the man associated the office building with the company for which he worked as a consultant. He identified the workmen's construction difficulties with his boss who, through mismanagement, kept undermining the company. How can that help the dreamer? Having a dream show you a scene of chaos with which you are all too well acquainted in your waking life is not helpful in itself. How are we to benefit from our dreams?

Bringing Dreams to Life

The task is to bring into our conscious life what the dream is offering. There are at least three steps in this process. In the first place, it means taking the dream seriously, as if it were a wise teacher who had something worthwhile to teach you. Write your dreams out, be open to them and give them a chance to speak. Interpreting our dreams is much like mining a rich mineral deposit: it requires patience, discipline, and hard work. Just because some dreams make no sense initially is no reason to dismiss them. Some dreams are too dense, fragmentary or cryptic to access, but most dreams will reward patient and attentive study. Often a dream may reveal its meaning only in the light of subsequent events or alongside other dreams you have. The most helpful attitude to bring to dream interpretation is expectancy.

Second, it means trying to become fully aware of what the dream is saying—actually experiencing it. This may be done by *feeling into* a dream, rather than just *thinking* about it. The technique of "active imagination," as described earlier, is that process of experiencing the dream. In a waking state, be in the dream again. Be aware of the relationships, the emotions, the energy in the various symbols or images. What does it feel like? In the case of the man who dreamed of the office building, it would be a matter of feeling what it is like from inside the dream, from the dreamer's point of view, as if he were invested in the building and at risk by its collapse. How does he feel toward the boss whom he believes is responsible for mismanagement? By fully developing these feelings, he will become aware of what is important to him in the dream. In the case of this building dream, the dreamer would realize what is in danger that is valuable to him and how he feels about the cause of the difficulty. Such feelings might suggest a course of action that he wants to take. This step of getting inside the dream and feeling it consciously might be called "living the dream."

Third, it means incorporating into your waking life what you have discovered to be of value from the dream. This involves consciously deciding about the dream's message. It may mean making a decision about something in your daily life, or changing an attitude, or deciding just to let the dream awareness sit for a few days to "percolate." In the case of the business consultant, working on his dream in this way clarified his frustration in that work situation and confirmed for him how powerless he was to implement sound business practice over against his boss's mismanagement. As a result, he decided to back off and put his energy into other consulting jobs. In many ways, this is the most difficult step in finding benefit in dreams. It is the hard work of actually producing the dream insight into a life change. It involves challenging the *status quo* in yourself, of trying something new and perhaps unfamiliar, of thinking and acting differently toward yourself or others. It is the process of applying the new attitude or insight in action.

A few dreams seem to come with "how to use" instructions: they offer such explicit guidance that their application is obvious. The dreamer knows at once whether they refer, for example, to a decision that is pending, to the planning for a trip, or to a relationship issue. These belong to the first basic type of dream mentioned in the last chapter, dreams that seem to be replying to the day's events in an effort to find solutions and to consolidate our personal memory accordingly. But many dreams are not that clearly pointed and most of life's issues are not that simple or straightforward.

Individuation: The Process of Personal Transformation

Most dreams seem to be aiming at something deeper and more complex than immediate problem-solving. They are more involved with the process of helping us grow toward maturity and wholeness. Many of their themes refer to our inner life rather than our outer circumstances. They may help us become more integrated personalities, more centered and clear on who we are, more aware of our various feelings and values. Let us now look at how dreams work within our inner life to bring change and thus to help us grow toward wholeness.

The process of maturing is a matter of becoming the unique person you are. Just as acorns become oak trees, so each person has a destiny of becoming what she was meant to be. There is an unfolding of one's potentiality in which the person becomes aware and able to live out more fully the richness of her personality.

Such growth to our unique destiny is not automatically assured, however. In the course of developing to adulthood, we all encounter obvious pressures, from parents, siblings, authority figures, and friends, to submerge or deny that uniqueness. In relating to the demands and expectations of others, each person faces countless decisions about conformity. Out of a need for acceptance, or even survival, therefore, the child may have denied his essential nature and complied with the demands of the situation. Thus a "false self" formed, complete with polished roles and pleasing behavior, which was untrue to the person's inner being.

In contrast, the movement toward maturity is the process by which the "true self" of the person unfolds toward its unique destiny. Jung called this process "individuation." He spoke of it as a matter of embracing "our innermost, last and incomparable uniqueness" and of "coming to 'self-hood' or 'self-realization.'"[19]

Much of our experience tells us that this process of finding our true identity comes through interacting with the outer world of people and things. This is particularly so in the early years of our life. Through childhood, adolescence and young adulthood, we often have the sense that it is largely our social relationships that give us our identity. It is a matter of making conscious decisions toward outer things, such as friends, career, a mate.

But when we look deeper, and especially as we grow older, we come to understand that there is an inner source of maturity. Some people are fortunate enough to move through to maturity smoothly and easily. Often, however, we only become aware of the inner path to maturity when the outer world fails us in some crucial way: the job we used to find stimulating loses its appeal; we develop an illness that jolts us; activities with friends become boring; or marriage seems lifeless or faded. Frequently, it is not until well into mid-life that we realize that we have no energy for some outer contacts that used to come so naturally: it seems that who we are in the outer world is at odds with how we have come to feel in our heart. All of this underlines the fact that true satisfaction lies in finding a harmonious relationship between our inner and outer worlds. This is where individuation, the growth to wholeness, depends on revealing what lies in the unconscious part of ourselves.

The fullest sense of self-realization takes place when the conscious part of ourselves, the ego, learns from the unconscious and grows by receiving into consciousness the inner truth that lies hidden in the unconscious. Jung believed that this process is the basis of human destiny:

> Man's task is...to become conscious of the contents that press upward from the unconscious. Neither should he persist in his unconsciousness, nor remain identical with the unconscious elements of his being, thus evading his destiny, which is to create more and more consciousness. As far as we can discern, the sole purpose of human existence is to kindle a light in the darkness of mere being.[20]

This process of making the unconscious conscious is the heart and soul of Jung's understanding of personal transformation, what Marie-Louise von Franz, one of Jung's closest associates, called "his myth for our time." It seemed to him that all personal transformation, indeed the advancement of humanity as a species, depended upon human consciousness being enlarged and enriched by the emergence of knowledge and energy that was previously unknown and held in the unconscious.

According to this view, the conscious part of ourselves grows by receiving resources from within. These may be in the form of new discoveries, new feelings, attitudes, strengths, and values that enlarge our conscious personality. For example, a middle-aged woman who had had an alcoholic mother and an emotionally distant father struggled with feelings of emptiness. She never felt she belonged or was loved. It was an agony for her to trust any intimate relationship. She often doubted her worth and struggled to identify what she really wanted for herself. Working with her dreams put her in touch with another dimension of her life. Slowly, over a period of years, she found how images of empty houses and lonely journeys, which corresponded to the abandonment experiences of her childhood, gave way to dreams of encounters with real people who were involved with her in a mutually interactive way. The images of her dreams began to express her identification with people who gave her a sense of worth and belonging. One such dream involved her in a rural scene in which she was riding on a donkey with Mary, the mother of Jesus, holding her as a baby and with Joseph walking nearby. By receiving the feeling of that image, and making it part of her conscious awareness, she was strengthened. She experienced the warmth of a different kind of mother than she had had. As a result, she had a more confident sense of her worth as a person. This is but one instance of an extended process by which something whole was created in her emptiness through the material that dreams gave and through the therapeutic relationship we had. In such ways dream images connect us to the unconscious and its resources.

Earlier we suggested that some dreams could be understood solely from a conscious standpoint, that at least one meaning was relatively obvious. Why, then, is the unconscious so important to the individuation process? In the first place, because the conscious mind is limited. There is so much it does not know. The information explosion that has taken place in this century has vastly expanded our knowledge, yet every increase in knowledge makes us more aware of how much we do not know and how we are dwarfed by the realities we study. Jung would go further and say that what we do know has come through the gradual emergence of consciousness out of unconsciousness. All we have to make sense of the universe lies in our consciousness. For future growth, we are dependent upon what is presently unknown becoming conscious.

In the second place, the unconscious is important for our growth to maturity because the conscious mind is fragmented and conflicted. It is in need of healing. Who is not aware of his own divided nature, inconsistencies, fears and frailties? Of course, the "success" culture in which we live pretends a pretty picture. Seeing a person securely functioning in a role that he has mastered, as a mechanic, classroom teacher, manager, or TV personality, for example, you might not guess those times when he is desperately lonely or afraid or gripped with terrible self-doubt. If we are honest with ourselves, most of us have times when we are on the ropes, though we may hide them by keeping a tight rein on our emotions and by wearing a practiced smile. We are consummate actors. Yet, to ourselves, we cannot deny the solitary night watches at 4 a.m. when all the world around is asleep except ourselves and we must come to terms with those things that never sleep and refuse to leave us alone. What is it that wakes us up or that will not be soothed away by any amount of frantic work or the escapism of drugs or alcohol? The ego struggles with its limits and loneliness, its conflicts and complexes and, if not in search of help, at least is in need of it.

We have spoken of the need to grow toward maturity which is each person's personal journey. In this process, consciousness with its center in the ego is not enough. It needs the resources of that larger reality, the unconscious. In the third place, then, the unconscious is so important because it contains images and symbols which can bring wholeness to the fragmented ego-personality.

How Dreams Bring Wholeness

Dreams as Compensation

In the foregoing, we have spoken of how ego-consciousness is limited, fragmented and in conflict. In this situation of need, dreams function for wholeness by compensating the ego from out of the resources of the unconscious. Compensation is the process of altering the structures of the ego to bring it toward fulfilment in union with the Self. Jung said that the goal of individuation is to bring the ego to surrender to the Self, that is, to find its true strength in relationship to that higher and greater source of being. Dreams function in this process by assisting in changing the limited view of the waking ego in line with the larger view of the whole psyche. Compensation may take four forms.

(1) Dreams express repressed material.

The unconscious contains material that has been repressed or forgotten for whatever reason, as well as material at the deeper archetypal level which has never been conscious. The repressed material may be something quite foreign to the usual conscious value or expression of the person. It may, for example, be something too violent or angry, crude or hurtful, to be accepted into normal waking expression. As a means of defense, such contents have been split off from consciousness and forgotten. If healing is to take place, however, it is necessary to work through and overcome that separation. Dreams provide a way of doing that. When the time is right for the ego to benefit from the forgotten material which the conscious mind has not allowed itself to embrace, dreams may reintroduce it into consciousness as a means of overcoming the separation between those two parts of the person. The dream gives a safe forum for those difficult feelings to take shape and to be accepted into the person's conscious awareness. Dreams compensate or help fulfil the ego by expressing contents that have been split off from consciousness and forgotten.

An instance of such repression may be seen in the dreams of a woman whose development was frustrated by a broken marriage. Now, in her early forties, she had suffered much through a long painful marital separation that had not resolved into a divorce settlement which might have permitted her to get on with her life. She had a series of dreams filled with violence: there were recurrent images of men who had been murdered or persons killed in car accidents. It made no sense to her. Consciously, she was a very decent, born-again Christian who said she had forgiven her estranged husband and had friendly relationships with both men and women. But the dreams identified intensely angry feelings within her that needed some expression. They compensated for the denial and tight conscious control she usually kept on these feelings. By coming repeatedly in her dreams, these violent images were prompting her to acknowledge her anger and to express it appropriately.

(2) Dreams "objectify" unconscious contents.

One way in which the dream adds to a person's consciousness is by objectifying something that was previously unknown. It states a situation in a way that the dreamer can see it objectively, apart from his usual attachment to it. The dream of the business troubleshooter, mentioned earlier (pp. 141–142), shows this process at work. His dream set out the problem of behind-the-scenes undermining of the whole business edifice in the image of the impressive facade of the building and the frantic and failing efforts of the workmen. It is as if the dream puts this dilemma out there on a TV screen for the man to see, and to decide about. It seems to be saying to him: Look squarely at this situation of your work. What do you see? Now, what are you going to do about it?

Edward Edinger speaks of this kind of process as a "mirror function." He gives the example of a man in the early stages of analysis who dreamed that he looked into a mirror and was amazed to see that his face was his father's face.

The dream was a mirror enabling him to see the fact (that he was identified with his father)—to make his identification with his father an object of knowledge. Thus the subject of knowledge (the ego) became separated from the object of knowledge (identification with his father), and the dreamer took his first step out of that identification and into greater consciousness.[21]

It would be typical in the early stages of analysis for a person to be involved in persona work such as this. It sounds as if this man, with the help of his dream, was beginning to see the difference between his own ego and a role (persona) he was playing as his father. Previously his ego had identified with that persona. But the dream, by objectifying the identification, enabled him to separate his perception of himself from his perception of his father. Now he could see and feel the difference.

This kind of identification is similar to a mechanism called "projection." That is, we project onto others aspects of ourselves so that we see those persons not as they are but through a filter of our own experience which distorts the truth about them. For example, we may see someone as a frightening authority because he walks or talks in a way that resembles someone whom we actually did fear for his authority. That is only a problem when it is unconscious, that is, when we actually believe the projection and don't realize that we are doing it. As in the case of the man who identified with his father, the first step in unmasking projections is to recognize the difference between what we see that is really the other person and what is coming from within ourselves (projections). Then, by owning these projections and pulling them back, we begin to see others the way they are and to know ourselves as we really are.

This process is a basic stage in marriage: once the honeymoon is over, we may begin to discover ways in which our partner is different than what we had expected. It is then that, instead of leaving, we might begin to recognize the projections we may have placed on them. The objectivity of that discovery may allow us to own as part of ourself what we had projected and to have a more realistic relation with our mate.

Incidentally, dreams of mirror images or of things that are twinned may often indicate something that is just coming into consciousness and may be about to happen.

(3) Dreams "balance" onesideness in the personality.

Consciousness is not the complete story as to who we are. Usually there are other dimensions and expressions of ourselves that are opposite to, or different from, how we see ourselves consciously. The "shadow" side of our personality is one way to speak of these hidden or unknown identities within us. They tend to balance the conscious part that has been dominant but is only one part of the truth about us.

Frequently, we find that dreams present a less complimentary side of ourselves to balance a proud or inflated ego; but what emerges from the unconscious may just as easily be a corrective to a deflated or defeated ego. This latter situation was so for a single woman suffering from depression who became aware of a pattern to her mood swings. "I have begun to notice," she said, "that, when I become hopeful about making possible changes and begin to feel enthused about my possibilities, something comes along and sweeps it all away before I can actually do anything to change." I replied, "Sounds like you were never permitted to do anything you wanted to do." She explained that in her family growing up she never saw anyone ever taking charge of their life or making intentional changes to improve their lot: it was simply survival. Where, then, had she gotten the notion of a better life for herself and the changes she wanted to make? Without a moment's hesitation she replied, "From my dreams." So dreams may supply the much-needed positives to a person whose conscious life has been bleak.

By offering images that complement or balance the conscious sense a person has of herself, dreams fill out a more complete range of personality. A good instance of that may be seen in the case of the woman whose fairly puritan sense of her sexuality was altered and enlarged by the earthy dream image of "Juanita," the Spanish prostitute. The resulting balance was more harmonious and natural for both her and her husband.

(4) Dreams "amplify" conscious material.

Because symbols operate on different levels of meaning at the same time, they are a means of enlarging narrow meanings and enriching our understanding. Things that previously had only one level of meaning now open up to various levels, which enrich the original meaning. An instance of an amplified meaning would be where a dream could be applied both subjectively (to oneself) and objectively (to a known person or image). For example, a woman dreamed that she was attending a party being held at her aunt's home. Many people were there including her own mother, but the aunt was prominent. In waking life, the dreamer had little to do with her aunt and could not understand why she would be dreaming about her. Then it came out that the aunt had a very strong personality and was able to look after herself well in relation with her husband, something that the dreamer's mother had not done in her marriage. Who was the dreamer more like in this regard, her mother or her aunt? Without question, the dreamer was like her aunt in this, but until recently had been passive, like her mother, in relation to men. Here the dream seemed to offer several meanings at once: it showed how the dreamer's mother and aunt were quite different in regard to how they related to men; it portrayed the aunt's strength of character; it revealed an attraction that focused in the aunt (the many people, representing energy, gathered in the party scene) suggesting that the dreamer was drawn to the aunt. In the associations afterward, the dreamer recognized that she and her aunt were similar in regard to this strength of personality, but that she was not applying that actively in her relationship with the man in her life. So the message of a dream could be true for the person dreamed about, in this case the aunt, and, at the same time, that person might represent some characteristic which is also true of the dreamer. One of the values of such an understanding would be to make the dreamer aware of that common factor and to point to the aunt figure as a model for her.

Ralph's "Border Crossing" dream, cited earlier in chapter 8, offers another example of the way in which dream symbols not only complement and balance conscious meanings but add to and integrate meanings into a rich whole. The symbol of the ridge of rock on the Canadian side of the border has the initial sense of some barrier reinforcing a boundary line. That suggests defensiveness when we realize that it is fortified along the top with a jagged edge and that Ralph, in working on the dream, experiences himself hiding behind the wall. But Ralph is only a tourist in the dream and is then involved in the rather neutral task of locating a marker on the outer side of the wall that coincides with his inner position. This observing and locating activity seems to relate to the process of analysis in which he was involved.

However, the symbols in the dream open Ralph up to various levels and sides of his dilemma. The inner and outer markings represent two positions or viewpoints The inner certainly stands for his withdrawal into a defensive stance. The urgency of keeping his inner position hidden is heightened by the fact that those on the outside are searching to locate the point opposite his inner position, with the sense that there could then be an opening made which would connect inner and outer. One of his images is that someone from the U.S. side is using a long pointer for this purpose. Such an image takes on special significance when one makes the connection that as an infant Ralph was given a series of enemas and he associates this with his fear of forced intimacy. Could the pointer represent an enema or the analytical process, or both?

The U.S. in Ralph's dream also opens to various levels of meaning. Considering its position in the dream, it could represent observing outsiders whom Ralph experienced as threatening. Taken with the pointer, it could represent a "foreign invasion"; taken with Ralph's association of a "promised land," and with his analytical interest in overcoming the split within himself, it could represent his coming out into a harmonious relationship. Considering his association of U.S. with "us," it might mean the possibility of uniting his separated parts. Only Ralph can say which of these holds for him at this point in his self-understanding.

We may see from the multi-level meaning of dream symbols how dreams function to offer connections which may not have been conscious previously, and how they function to enlarge conscious meaning and to integrate it so that things that didn't seem to fit become connected.

The Role of Archetypes in Individuation

The unconscious functions in a dialogue with consciousness to transform the ego and bring it to wholeness. In this process, in which the ego-consciousness receives material from the unconscious and integrates it into consciousness, it is important that the ego be strong enough to take on the unconscious material. For one thing, dream interpretation goes better when we have a well-defined, realistic sense of who we are. It anchors us from being lost in a fantasy world. No matter how intriguing the images of dreams may be or how enchanting the worlds they spin, it is important that we remain rooted in the real world of consciousness and keep relating the dream material back to the situation of our waking state. Psychosis may occur when consciousness is overwhelmed by the unconscious, that is, when the ego cannot distinguish between reality and unreality. When working with dreams, therefore, it is important to be sure of a strong ego and to spend some time developing its strength.

In doing analysis, I find it helpful in the early stages, or when in doubt about a person's ego strength, to undertake a process of ego-building. This may involve exercises to help a person identify and claim personal strengths. Skills, abilities, accomplishments, as well as personality traits, physical attributes, matters of moral and spiritual character are listed as "I am" or "I have" self-affirmations. Then these positive qualities are claimed aloud and may be repeated on a daily basis. In addition, I give support for the person's decision-making, and validation of the person's expressed needs and realistic viewpoints. If you are not in analysis but working on your own dreams, I would strongly recommend that you practice this kind of self-affirmation, before you go more deeply into your dreams.

We turn now to consider the key role which archetypes play in the individuation process. By bringing its own unique symbols to consciousness, each archetype contributes an aspect of wholeness to the growing ego.

Persona:

As dreams depict the various roles the dreamer plays and those become conscious, the person may be able to feel the difference between his ego and the various personas. A professional woman who struggled with a very masculine, achievement-driven ego provides a good example of individuation through persona differentiation. She came to me initially to cope with cancer. Her excessive workaholism had led her to illness and the brink of exhaustion. The illness itself had forced her to become conscious of how her self-worth had been tyrannized by the need to achieve. Her dreams had shown her driving her own car at high speeds and gave images from her work-life role that portrayed her as overloaded and enslaved by having to achieve. As she began consciously to work at changing this attitude toward work, she had a dream in which the image of a spinning wheel appeared. It made little sense until the connection was made to the treadle and the archetypal sense of the easy rhythm of a woman's foot spinning the thread of life. It offered a totally different sense of work. Whereas her habitual persona was one of hard-driving, achievement-oriented work, geared to meeting external expectations, this new persona was attuned to an inward rhythm that was more natural and humane. Not only did it offer her a new attitude toward her work role, it also, by contrast, made her more conscious of the destructiveness of her original work-style. She could see two different ways of being: the natural fluctuating rhythm of the treadle, issuing in the steady spinning of the wheel, an essentially

feminine way of being, and the high-powered racing of
her car, drivenness, masculinity at its most stressful.

Differentiating in this way can be very helpful for the
person who is then enabled to be intentional in choosing
a persona activity rather than playing one out uncon-
sciously. The person's ego identity is thereby enhanced
and made more authentic, while the roles played are freed
from being social impositions. The result is an ego whose
repertoire has been enlarged and enriched by personas,
rather than being entrapped in roles that are imposed and
therefore inauthentic or phoney.

Shadow:

As the shadow begins to be received into consciousness
through dream images, the conscious ego-identity is
confronted by its opposite or contrary tendencies.
Initially, shadow images can be offensive to the ego and
may be met with skepticism or even with outright denial,
as Juanita, the Spanish prostitute, was in the dream
mentioned earlier. But as the ego becomes stronger and
able to tolerate more conflict, shadow images become
more acceptable, even humorously welcome. What is
often most convincing is the increased energy and
balance the person feels in his conscious sense of himself.
The shadow offers potentiality to the ego and so its
acceptance comes to be greeted with enthusiasm.

Animus-anima:

Through the animus-anima, the person may come to be
joined to the collective unconscious. Presentation of the
animus-anima in dreams offers a potential love
relationship to the ego. This may range from images of
friendship and emotional support to sexual passion and
love. Examples may be found in my dream of "my"
woman who took me to the dress shop and modelled the

marvellous scarlet and white dress in front of me (pp. 132–133). Jung often spoke of the anima as the man's soul, the animus as the woman's spirit. Dreams showing a positive relationship of the animus-anima with the dream-ego bring inner harmony and even what Jung called "the marriage of the soul." However, there may be negative animus-anima images which present the ego with a frightening or unfulfilling contra-sexual connection and raise questions of where such unloving images might have arisen.

Self:

The ego and the Self are in a unique relationship in that they are twin foci of the core of the person, the ego being the conscious center and the Self the unconscious, divine center. The way they relate to each other is crucial for the well-being of the person. Generally, there is a basic correspondence of the conscious to the unconscious personalities of the person so that the Self represents the true fulfilment of the ego.

The connection between the ego and the Self is known as "the ego-Self axis." Edward Edinger[22] has depicted the ego-Self axis as shown in Figure 4. (Here the larger circle represents the unconscious part of the individual with the Self as center, and the smaller circle represents the individual's consciousness with the ego as center.) He identifies the ego-Self axis as the fundamental relationship for maturity, maturity being the greatest extension of the ego-Self axis into consciousness. What is shown in this figure are progressive stages in ego-Self development. The shaded areas represent the residual identity the ego has with the Self, the unshaded part of ego-consciousness represents the extent of individuation. The axis line connecting the ego-center with the Self-center is "the vital connecting link between ego and Self that ensures the

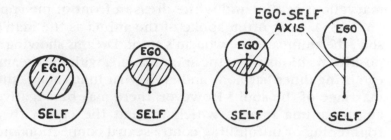

FIGURE 4

integrity of the ego." Thus, the more one becomes a unique individual yet remains conscious of one's connection to the Self, that is, the longer that axis grows while still maintaining contact, the more complete a person's individuation. Being in contact with the Self paradoxically empowers and produces a growing humility. Ultimately, the goal of individuation is to bring the developed ego to surrender to the Self.

Individuation and the Process of Ego Development

What wasn't mentioned explicitly in the above discussion of how archetypes function in individuation is that they provide a foundation and fulfilment for the complexes. Each complex is built around a core meaning that is rooted in a corresponding archetype. Just as the ego corresponds to, and finds its fulfilment in the Self, so the complexes find their essential completion in the archetypes.

In order to grasp how archetypes and complexes function in the individuation process, picture a three-level model of the individual psyche, consciousness above, personal unconscious beneath, and collective unconscious at the bottom. The individuation process takes place between the interaction of the ego, which is the center of consciousness, and the Self, which is the center of the whole psyche and is unconscious. Between the two, in the personal unconscious, are the complexes. (Again, let me emphasize that such attempts to schematize psychological factors are not meant to suggest a linear or spatial reality but are used only to give a sense of relationship. The psychological entities involved are intangible.)

Now we are ready to see how dreams function in the process of individuation. Some of the ego's struggle may be traced to the fact of limited consciousness which needs to benefit from the balancing and fulfilling influences of archetypes, as we have mentioned above. So a major way in which dreams function in individuation is by bringing the great symbols of the collective unconscious into consciousness to do their restorative work on the ego. But much of the ego's difficulty comes from distortions emanating from complexes that are rooted in the personal unconscious, which comes between the ego and the collective unconscious. Neurotic and even psychotic symptoms may be traced to the effect of powerful complexes which disrupt ego-functioning often without the person's awareness. Here are the irrational fears, projections, inferiority feelings, obsessions, and addictions that rob the ego of its power and obscure the ordering wholeness of the archetypes. In this situation, dreams function as part of what Jung called the "self-healing" process of the psyche. Dreams are able to give symbols representing the Self or other archetypes which correspond to the complexes and, by correcting their distortions, offer a way of taking the power out of a complex.

To illustrate, a familiar symbol for a mother complex may be a building that has a collective, security aspect to it, such as a government building, barn or a shopping mall. We may even call such buildings a complex. The man-made, enclosing and collective features represent the protective, sheltering and group-cohesive qualities embodied in the complex. Equally, the way in which individuality is sacrificed to institutional security is evident in the conformity and womb-likeness of the building. Dreams with such symbols often are addressing the complex-bound ego in its struggle to be free of fear and insecurity and to step out and risk independence and individuality. A man with such a mother complex found during the course of analysis and much suffering that his dream images entered a phase when such buildings were under demolition. Gigantic earthworks projects were being undertaken at the city center in which great mounds of earth were being turned up. New roads and building construction were underway. Symbols of other types of buildings, individual houses, sacred buildings or personalized chapels, and natural scenes, began to take the place of the complex symbols. The shift of image from collective to personal, as well as the demolition of old buildings and creation of new buildings and roads, together with more natural scenes, indicated an emphasis on his individual freedom and personal identity.

We never can be rid of our complexes—they make us the unique people we are—but we can change our attitude toward them so they no longer have the dominance they once had. This may be accomplished by making the ego more aware of the complex, by strengthening the ego so as not to be so helpless before the complex, and by giving the ego an experience of the truth of a reality in the unconscious that is deeper and more whole than the complex. For example, a negative mother complex that keeps criticizing and picking at the self-esteem of a woman from within may be put in perspective by dream symbols reflecting the Great Mother archetype filled with radiant love and holding the woman in her arms with delight; or a claustrophobic complex may be offset by images of the power and total adequacy of the Self.

Complexes, then, may be considered to be distortions of archetypal reality. Just as the ego finds its fulfilment in relationship to the Self, so the complexes must be set within the context and influence of the archetypes. The self-healing of the individual psyche requires that the ego be open to the resources of the unconscious as expressed in the archetypal symbols of dreams.

11
HOW IS THIS PRACTICAL FOR DAILY LIVING?

In this book we have presented a brief method of dream analysis and sketched the outline of a theory to explain how dreams work. I want now to show the practical benefit of using dreams for personal growth and daily living. Doing dream work could be seen as a kind of escapism into a fairy tale world that has no connection with real life. Especially when it involves delving into obscure symbols from antiquity or the mysteries of alchemy, it could be dismissed as just the hobby of a small elite. The point of view that I hope has been clear in what has been presented here is that dreams are of great practical value in everyday living.

Indeed, in my own experience I would say that dreams have become essential for my personal growth and well-being. Let me share an early experience of working with dreams that convinced me of their practical benefit. In the course of a household move, something went in my lower back as I jumped down from the truck. The pain was manageable and I thought it would soon heal, but the condition did not let up. Medical examinations and x-rays found nothing wrong and treatments, including chiropractic, proved ineffective. After several months in continuing pain which apparently had no physical foundation, I entered Jungian analysis. As we worked on my dreams and talked out the issues of my life, slowly the pain diminished and went away completely after six months. In place of the pain, I became aware of something that had been wrong in a basic relationship of my life, but which I had been avoiding. What I found then and have continued to find in other situations is that dreams are sources of wisdom for problem solving and life enhancement. They put us in touch with dimensions of ourselves that are normally hidden and that we need in order to grow toward our full potential.

One of the most practical benefits of dream work is how it reveals these unknown aspects of our personality, that are closed to us in our waking life, and makes them available. It can be vitally important that we understand what lies within us. A woman who had been diagnosed with cancer of the breast worked intensively for seven weeks using relaxation, visualization, life-style counselling, prayer and dream analysis until a second test was done which showed "only scar-tissue." Two days later she had a dream in which she was the only observer at a dress rehearsal. On the stage was a large wooden cross from which a noose hung, with a trap door beneath. "Surely they're not going to show that (execution)!" she said to herself. The only figure on stage was a fat man with his coat collar pulled up hiding his face. She could hear him chortling with delight. In discussing the dream, she said it referred to her possible death, and that she regarded treatment by either radiation or surgery as a kind of "double death." When I asked about the man who was on stage, she said he was delighted with the prospect of the coming death. She understood that figures in dreams could represent parts of oneself, so I asked was there a part of her like that man? "Yes, he's my cynic."

Up to that point, the woman had vigorously maintained that she wanted to live and believed that she could survive the cancer. This was the first indication that there was an unconscious part of her that did not want to get well again. Coming, as the dream did, shortly after the second medical test, it's message was clearly from that cynical part that doubted the good report. That awareness of a negative attitude, which could be classed as a death wish, gave us a focus for our work over the next several months. It permitted us to engage consciously in the battle between her negative and positive attitudes toward life. Incidentally, she is very much alive twelve years later.

In dreams, we enter a state of knowledge that is closed to us in our waking life, but which is vital to our growth and well-being. By giving us entrance to those additional resources, dreams aid in the process by which we may go forward in life. Indeed they may lead us into a new phase of life. The following is such a dream which a workshop participant volunteered to analyze with me in front of the group. She did so with some reluctance because of the group exposure, but also with little expectation that the dream would unfold such hopeful new vistas as it did.

Dream Study #1

Dorothy is a woman in her early 40's who has been divorced for five years. She had been emotionally burnt both in her marriage, in which she felt severely criticized by her ex-husband, and in the aftermath of the divorce, when she felt betrayed by both family and friends. As a result, over the last two years, she had pulled back into herself, maintaining only a facade with others and not giving as she once had. She found herself searching for her own identity through university studies, journalling, dreams and art.

Dorothy's Dream:

First, I had a brief dream of being in an elevator which is going up and down. I am trying to get off at the right floor and finally do get off. I think I get off at a higher floor than I got on.

The second dream is much clearer and longer. I walk along a grassy area in a garden with Sam's (my ex-roomate's) friend and have a conversation about a divorced couple, in which the woman is older than the man, and about how the young man is attracted to the older woman. I think it's too bad the couple is breaking up after twenty years. My attitude toward Sam's friend is "pleasing"—that is, I hope he will find me attractive. We walk up the steps to where there is a stone hedge and huge lily leaves. They reach out to me as if to give me something. They seem to know me. I rub the leaves and they have a fragrance. Millions of tiny seeds suddenly appear. I have an "aha" experience—one of joy and wonder.

Content

1. The Setting:
Garden/landscape

2. The Images: (objects, animals, people, forms)

Sam's friend	stone hedge	old couple, divorced
leaves	seeds	woman older than man,
grass	lily leaves	young man attracted to
		older woman

3. The Main Theme:
Discovering where the gift is

4. The Action or Effect:

Walking through garden area with Sam's friend. I ask, "Why have they broken up after so many years?" The young man is interested in an older woman. I rub the leaf and it has a fragrance. Some of the leaves will hold the seeds that fall.

5. The Feeling Tone in the Dream:

Longing, wonder, curiosity

Context

6. The Feeling on Waking:

Confused, but feel like I had received a gift.

7. Previous Day's Events:

Work, a writing lab, talking with two women friends, dream workshop. Anxiety about not doing enough.

8. Emotional Landscape:

a. What emotional focus was there the day before the dream?

Fear of being judged; fear of not being productive enough, not doing enough at work; fear of having to resolve others' difficulties—not up to it. I want freedom!

b. What emotionally charged issues lay ahead?

Course work and an essay that is due (fear of being judged inadequate).
Ongoing concerns re: lack of energy, swollen glands.

Associations

9. What associations do you have to any of the images in the dream?

    couple=Mom and Dad, divorced after twenty years
seeds=hope?
lily=plants of my first garden
leaves=palms of hands in prayer, cupped
leaves in shape of mandorla (an almond- or leaf-shaped religious crest). I had drawn a leaf in my journal the night before when questioning another dream image about jewels growing on my throat.
    Sam's friend=an electrician, nice, lonely, hard worker, goes unnoticed

10. What in your life has been similar to elements in the dream?
    — had garden this year
    — would find older woman/younger male curious
    — my ex-husband was younger than I
    — looking for the "seeds of truth"
    — desire to be rooted?

11. What memories does the dream bring back?
    Mom and Dad's divorce
    Fears of being unattractive
    Desire for attention from males
    Rhode Island

12. What similarities does this dream have to other dreams you've had? To religious or secular stories, legends or fairy tales?

    Aladdin's Lamp—the sense of a magical gift being

offered—the lamp has to be rubbed, as I feel I also have to do something

Amplification

13. Balance:

a. How is this dream different than your waking attitude or values?

In my waking life I am not attracted to Sam's friend, but in the dream I find him quite attractive.

In the dream I have a people-pleasing quality that I don't admire in waking life.

b. What conscious attitude might this dream be trying to balance or compensate?

I sometimes feel isolated, alone and empty, and doubtful about life's purpose. This dream suggests that something greater is listening.

I can get lost in doing, working and thinking. The dream shows me the need to get in touch with physical, natural reality; with touch and smell.

c. What does it add to your usual way of living or thinking?

It reinforces my connection to nature. In my workaday world I allow myself to be dominated by logic and what I would call a "masculine" way of thinking and acting. But that is really foreign to me and has raised doubts in me about what and who I can trust. Nature is different. It is my usual way of living. Because in the dream I was presented with the gift by nature, I feel I can trust what nature gives me. Sometimes I forget this and here the dream gives me a reminder.Also, it brings me to talk about my true nature.

16. Draw or sculpt the dream: What insights or discoveries came out for you?

When I drew the dream I became more aware of the intense feeling of nature—the grassy area, the stone hedge, the lily leaves so verdant and out-reaching, the seeds coming down, about to land and take root. It emphasized the importance of nature to me. The seeds also remind me of a type of drawing that I do just using dots, but with them creating an image and effect by the way they cluster and shade.

18. What question might this dream be answering?

Do I have the courage to accept and use my gifts?

21. Archetypal identity: What evidence is there of the presence of transpersonal or archetypal connection in the dream?

The shape of the leaves and seeds were reminiscent of the mandorla—a symbol that is almond-shaped, usually having the figure of Christ in the center, sometimes surrounded with four apocalyptic figures, representing the four evangelists. Although I don't believe in organized religion, this information re the mandorla as a symbol of the divine is familiar to me from study of Gothic cathedrals and medieval symbols. The mandorla is often depicted on the portals leading into cathedrals, especially early Gothic cathedrals. I had a sense of some divine offering being made to me by the leaves that held out their "hands" with seeds for me.

22. New Knowledge: What does this dream tell you about yourself and others that you did not know before?

When I explored the images of the leaves and the seeds being offered to me, I felt this may have to do with my divine gift, believing that each individual has a divine gift that is theirs to use in life. Through their gift, the divine is manifested. It is our task in life to sort through the collective "you should do this ...you should do that" to try and discover that essential gift that demands expression in our life. This is a question that has occupied my thoughts for years. With its natural setting, I think the dream is talking about my true nature and, especially, that the leaves made an offer to me—not just with the fragrance and the seeds—but by the gesture of offering—a gesture often seen in Christian paintings (e.g., presentation of gifts by the Magi). The association of the leaves and seeds to the mandorla further confirms for me the sense of divine gift. I feel that something is being given to me that is my own essential gift.

What that gift might be became clearer through this dream. The leaves and seeds in the dream reminded me of almond-shaped jewels which had been in a dream I had had some time ago. In that previous dream, jewels were around my neck, not like a necklace on the outside, but were actually part of my body, under the skin by my throat. When I was asked what in my life could be like those jewels, I immediately remembered that, earlier in my life, my singing voice had been recognized as a gift. I had even taken singing lessons with the prospect of a singing career ahead of me, but had stopped five years ago. Perhaps singing is a gift I want to re-cultivate now.

The presence of the electrician (Sam's friend) may be implying that my energy is increasing or that I am trying to attract the right kind of energy to myself. This makes sense to me, since I have been fighting a fatigue that has seriously interfered with my life. The seeds could symbolize new growth, new fertilization, or something that is in the "air" about to land and take root.

23. Conscious Response: What question, action, or decision do you want to make in response to this dream?

I want to reconnect with nature.

I want to discover what new life is being offered me in the seeds. As part of that, I want to develop my singing.

Postscript:

"As a result of the dream, I have taken the following actions: (1) I have consciously focused on music and singing. I have made more of an effort to sing at home. I have started buying music and have been thinking of buying an instrument. I realize that music is partly where my soul is. (2) Although I feared being judged, I took courage and acted on something that was emotionally packed and wrote the course paper that I feared writing. I got a high A grade on it and 92% on the course. My ideas do make sense!"

Dorothy went on to say that a week after having the dream she met a man several times in a purely professional setting, but she kept thinking about him afterwards in connection with the dream. It provoked a real debate within her, because she hadn't consciously been wanting a relationship. Finally, she came to the decision that she could accept someone in her life again and wondered if the dream had somehow pointed her in that direction.

She concluded: "The interesting thing is that suddenly I have more energy, when for the last four or five years I have had to 'will' myself through every day struggling with extreme fatigue that would not be cured with any amount of sleep."

Comment: Dorothy's dream seemed to be a pivot on which she moved from the withdrawn, defiant person she had been following her divorce toward a life that was beginning to express itself with trust and creativity toward others. She experienced more energy and an end to the fatigue that had beset her. Of course, such a change cannot be credited to one dream, and is more likely a gradual process of growth over time. She had had the earlier dream of jewels by her throat and there may have been other dreams, insights and decisions which had their role in the positive change taking place. However, by her own account and in recounting her subsequent experience to me, she mentioned that ever since having this dream her mind kept flitting back to it as a special moment of meaning for her.

There are several factors in the dream itself that might explain why it had such a powerful influence on her. There was the undoubted impact of a divine gift being offered. It gave her a sense of being in touch with some transcendent power or purpose. This was reinforced by the important connection with nature as a feminine force which could be trusted. The image of the lily leaves reaching their "palms" out to her bearing seeds was compelling, and came as a welcome and total reversal of the negative and hurtful experiences that had dominated her experience throughout her marriage break-up and divorce. It seems to me that the image of the seeds has only begun to shed its meaning on her. They stand for potentiality itself. They were quickly associated with the jewels around her neck in her previous dream and brought her to identify her neglected singing gift as a source of new expression. But seeds might also represent fertilization and germination, as Dorothy mentioned in her associations, which could have wider implications.

The figure of Sam's friend also brings energy into her conscious life. This man who in conscious life does not attract her is quite different in her dream, suggesting that he is an animus figure, representing her inner connection to the masculine lover that she has lost in the outer world. By making that connection conscious and believable to her, the dream opens the way for her to trust again that she could accept someone (the right one?) again. Here is a good example of the way in which an archetype (in this case, an animus) can bring hope and healing to the conscious person. We can see here how the energy follows the image.

Dream Study #2

Just how practical dreams can be is shown in the case of a man whose dream, which was analyzed using the worksheet format, helped him to make an important life-decision.

Oscar was not happy in his marriage. With his wife he felt a lack of communication, understanding and intimacy. Sexual relations had diminished to the point where they had been celibate for more than a year.

During this time, a close relationship had developed with a woman at work. In that relationship, which was platonic, he found a spiritual companionship in which he experienced understanding, mental stimulation, a religious and spiritual bond, and an unconditional acceptance which was unique in his life.

For several months prior to our session, he had been experiencing the effects of an infection of his prostate gland which had resisted several attempts at antibiotic treatment. In reply to my question about what he thought might be causing this infection, he said he did not know but that it seemed connected to a hard cord or muscle that ran downward from below his navel to just above his pubic bone. It was hard and painful and he had been aware of it for at least four years.

He thought this painful muscle experience was associated with the conflicting forces which he felt were pulling him apart in that area: one force, the pull to freedom represented by this other woman, and the other force being his wife who held him down with practical realities and responsibility. He considered this holding down to be serving a good purpose, in that he tended to need that kind of grounding in the real world. He likened this conflict to the difference between blasting off like the Challenger space craft versus the pull of gravitation that kept one safely on the earth. He said the hard muscle kept him from exploding like Challenger into a thousand pieces.

It was at this point that he remembered a dream which he had had two months before at a time when he was seriously considering leaving his marriage.

Oscar's Dream: "The Oasis and The Garden Tools"

I am at my home (not my actual home, but I recognize that it is mine) and set out on a journey to an oasis I want to go to very much. It is one day's journey away and I set out hurriedly across the desert. Soon I realize that I have no water, but that doesn't seem important. Then I realize I have no hat and I will need a hat because the sun is so hot. I turn back to get my hat. When I arrive home, my wife is just coming back with our three children. She asks me how I paid for the garden tools I had just bought, and I tell her I paid by check. She asks how I could afford it. I feel some shame, like I was a bad boy, telling her I wrote a check for it.

Content

1. The Setting:

I was standing out behind my house (it was not the home I live in, but I knew it was mine) looking out at the vast expanse of desert that began on the other side of my property. There seemed to be almost a line where my grass ended and dropped off immediately into the desert.

2. The Images:

An oasis, out of sight over the sandy desert.

It was bright sunlight behind my white house.

Image of the oasis attracting me, although I couldn't actually see it.

My wife, children, wife's car, some garden tools, my check book.

3. The Main Theme:

My desire to follow my attraction to the oasis, but recognizing I needed my hat (and water) before going.

4. The Action or Effect:

I stop myself from heading out willy-nilly into the desert and then come home to discover there are a lot of practical aspects of life that I have not been thinking about.

5. The Feeling Tone in the Dream:

Excitement—exhilaration about heading out to the oasis—unfettered

Relief that I could restrain myself enough in my

enthusiasm to go back and get my hat to protect me from the sun and, since I was going back, to get a water bottle too.

Disappointment that my family was coming home again and that there were practical duties to be taken care of.

Hopelessness that all my wife seemed concerned about was the cost of the garden tools and where I got the money.

Context

6. *The Feeling on Waking:*

Exhilaration about the oasis and it being only one day's journey away. Pleased to remember the dream and sense that it was important for me.

7. *Previous Day's Events:*

I don't remember the specifics of the day.

8. *Emotional Landscape:*

a. *What emotional focus was there the day before the dream?*

Weighing whether to stay in my marriage or not.

Associations

9. *What associations do you have to any of the images in the dream?*

Oasis is freedom, salvation, healing, wholeness, "being in the valley of love and delight," a place of nurturance, of "living water," being connected to my potential by being grounded in love.

garden tools=work, duty, responsibility
husband=stewardship, responsibility

After working on the dream, I later realized that near the time of the dream I had made a sizeable financial investment for my children's future and that the check and paying the price represented my responsibility to them and the reluctance I had at the time to spending that much.

10. What in your life has been similar to elements in the dream?

The split I feel between the "leaper," free and venturesome, and the "dutiful" one.

12. What similarities does this dream have to other dreams you've had? To religious or secular stories, legends or fairy tales?

It reminded me of a dream in which I was chasing a very free woman out onto a boardwalk going out into the Mississippi River (or some very big, swift moving river). She slipped and ran and danced out farther and farther as the walk became skimpier and skimpier. She was fearless and I felt free following her, until I got to a place where I needed to stop and realized, if I went any farther, I could get killed falling off into this huge river. I pulled myself back just as I did in this dream when I got out into the desert and realized I didn't have my hat and that it would be reckless to go farther without it.

Amplification

13. Balance:

   a. How is this dream different than your waking attitude or values?

Unlike the dream, my conscious attitude is that I would probably need to leave the marriage at some point to have life.

14. Active Imagination: *(Go back into the dream and dialogue with any of the people, animals, objects.)*
What came out of the dialogue?

I dialogue with my wife in the dream and she says, "You seem oblivious to some of the practical details of life which are important. You take off on your great quest and forget the details."

15. Gestalt:

    a. How are you like the persons, animals, objects in the dream?

    b. What does it feel like to be that person, or object?

"I am the parched desert earth that is right behind your house and separates you from your oasis. I am very dry and empty and lifeless and barren and dead. I am totally dependent on what is done to me. In the spring, when it rains, all the needs in me are ignited into life and I am beautiful; but most of the year I look empty and forbidding. I look dead, but I'm not. If you get lost in me or are unprepared, I can kill you (not that I want to, but that's just the way it is). Many have died trying to cross me."

Now I realize that the desert represents my traumatized inner child. The road to the oasis goes through him. I know I have to get to know him, to go through his lifelessness, his pain and suffering, with him. Then, when the spring waters come, I can flower.

18. What question might this dream be answering?

What to do about my marriage? Don't go off half-cocked; don't go off without being aware of the practical aspects of your life. Now is not the time. You need to wait.

There is still this split in you, this division, which separates you from your healing.

You are not far off (only a day's journey) from your goal, salvation, healing.

19. Intervention: (Invite a religious figure or revered person into the dream scene and see what that person does with the situation.)

I invited Jesus into my dream. He said: "It will not be your willful or reckless abandon or your 'charge of the Light Brigade' that gets you to the oasis, but the gentle healing of my love for you which will give you your heart's desire."

22. New Knowledge: What does this dream tell you about yourself and others that you did not know before?

That the oasis is so near.

That what separates me from the freedom I desire is my traumatized inner child, symbolized by the desert. Previously I was trying to get across it, to pass over the wounded child experience. Now I see I have to go through it.

The dream made me more aware of the psychological split within myself between the practical and the spiritual and showed me that they are still quite separate. I realize now that they are separated by the traumatized child and that I need to get them together inside to really have my power.

23. Conscious Response: What question, action, or decision do you want to make in response to this dream?

I have decided to wait and not run recklessly out of the marriage.

Comment: Oscar's understanding of his dream grew and transformed as he worked with the dream analysis format. An early stage was the recognition that the dream expressed the alternatives of freedom (the oasis) and responsibility (home, family and checkbook). The parallel then came out between the oasis and garden tools in terms of both having to do with nurture and providing his basic needs from the earth: the oasis has plentiful water, vegetation and refreshment as gift; whereas the garden tools offer the same nurture, food and plenty from the earth, but require work. The oasis is all gift and seems like the unconditional acceptance of his woman friend, while the garden tools are associated with providing for his wife and family, and requires work. Later, as the dream analysis developed, he saw these two possibilities as being separated by the desert and, rather than being alternatives, they were two poles or focuses within himself that were separate and needed to be brought together.

The hat symbol was a key factor in showing him the need for integration of both freedom and responsibility. It symbolized survival and made him realize that he was being reckless in going out so impulsively. He recognized that in going back he was entering a more rational approach to his life, the hat being associated with his head and the thinking function.

On balance, it seemed that he did not want to abandon the marriage, because it was neither reasonable nor practical to do so. He had made two major discoveries from the dream which cast his dilemma in a new light. One was the awareness that the factor separating him from freedom was not his wife and family but the desert, his inner woundedness and desolation. He realized that the way to healing the split within himself between freedom and responsibility lay in tending to the needs of his wounded inner child. The other discovery was that the oasis was nearer than he had thought. The desert could be crossed in one day's journey. In that, there was some assurance that overcoming the desert may come soon. It was practical to stay and wait and work it through.

The beneficial influence of the dream continued to unfold for Oscar. Some six months after first working on the dream, Oscar reported that he had reflected on it frequently in the interim and had recognized he had not been taking full responsibility for family finances. As a result, he became more focused in his financial management, making some very practical investment decisions. Not only was he aware of the shift in his behavior, but also he felt good about acting differently. In terms of the dream, it seemed that the attitude of his wife in the dream was becoming more a part of his own conscious outlook.

Conclusion

Dreams need not give us answers as clearly as this one did for Oscar, in order to be a practical help for living. In far subtler ways, they assist in adding to consciousness and moving us toward wholeness. We may become impatient to find answers and to work through to solutions. But the truest kind of growth is that which goes beyond problem-solving. In one of his more profound moments, Jung said that we do not solve our problems, we outgrow them.

It is possible to take a too pragmatic stance to our dreams and expect that they will rescue us from difficult situations or provide ready-made solutions. There are no shortcuts to maturity. As all the masters and sages have told us in one way or another, the journey itself is the goal of our living. Life is not a problem to be solved, but a mystery to be lived. In that process, dreams offer companionship, encouragement and light.

NOTES

1. Stephen LaBerge, *Lucid Dreaming*.
2. Harry T. Hunt, *The Multiplicity of Dreams: Memory, Imagination, and Consciousness*.
3. Milton Kramer, *Dream Psychology and the New Biology of Dreaming*, p. 18.
4. Lawrence Le Shan, *Alternate Realities: The Search for the Full Human Being*, p. 18.
5. Morton T. Kelsey, *God, Dreams and Revelation: A Christian Interpretation of Dreams*, p. 14.
6. C. G. Jung, *Symbols of Transformation*, CW 5, par. 5.
7. E. A. Bennet,*What Jung Really Said*, p. 73.
8. David Foulkes, quoted in Hunt, *op. cit.*, p. 11.
9. C. G. Jung, *The Symbolic Life: Miscellaneous Writings*, CW 18, par. 135, 138.
10. Kelscy, *ibid.*, p. 53.
11. Patricia Garfield, *Creative Dreaming*.
12. C. G. Jung, *The Practice of Psychotherapy*, CW 16, par. 294.
13. Trudy Govier, "The Stuff That Dreams Aren't Made Of," *The Globe and Mail*, Toronto, December 8, 1992.
14. Wallace B. Clift,*Jung and Christianity*, p. 53; cf. p.13, and pp. 51 ff.
15. C. G. Jung, *The Structure and Dynamics of the Psyche*, CW 8, par. 45.
16. Wallace B. Clift, *ibid.*, p. 13.
17. Edward F. Edinger, "Psychotherapy and Alchemy," *Quadrant*, Summer, 1978.

18. Edward Whitmont, *The Symbolic Quest*, p. 291.
19. C. G. Jung, *Two Essays on Analytical Psychology*, CW 8, par. 266.
20. C. G. Jung, *Memories, Dreams, Reflections*, p. 326.
21. Edward F. Edinger, *The Creation of Consciousness*, p. 40.
22. Edward F. Edinger, *Ego and Archetype*, p. 5.

GLOSSARY

Anima: (Latin, "soul") The personification of the feminine nature of a man's unconscious. She is represented in dreams by a variety of images of women reflecting "all the ancestral...impressions ever made by woman" "engraved in the living organic system of the man"(Jung). She may manifest in a man's feeling, oversensitivity or moodiness.

Animus: (Latin, "spirit") Personification of the masculine nature of a woman's unconscious. The animus has the masculine character of being rational, goal-oriented and thinking. In it's unconscious form it is "a compound of spontaneous, unpremeditated opinions which exercise a powerful influence on the woman's emotional life" (Jung).

Archetypes: Universal patterns of human experience in the collective unconscious, having form but not content. When an archetype is expressed in an image which becomes conscious in a dream or vision, it takes on content and is then filled out with the material of conscious experience. Archetypes form the basic content of religions, legends, mythologies and fairy tales.

Complex: "Complexes are psychic fragments which have been split off owing to traumatic influences or certain incompatible tendencies" (Jung). They are bundles of emotionally charged ideas or images that have a

187

personality of their own and exert a disturbing influence on conscious performance.

Ego: The center of conscious personality; the seat of subjective identity.

Individuation: The maturing process whereby one becomes conscious of becoming one's unique self. It is a "coming to selfhood" or "self-realization."

Mandala: Magic circle, a symbol of the center or of the psychic process of centering. This centering aspect of the mandala is found in symbols of the circle, square, or quaternity and arrangements of the number four. These function to superimpose an order which holds chaotic elements together in a protective circle.

Persona: (Latin, "mask") "The persona...is the individual's system of adapation to, or the manner he assumes in dealing with, the world. Every calling or profession, for example, has its own characteristic persona" (Jung).

Self: The unifying and ordering center of the total psyche (conscious and unconscious); the seat of objective reality. The "inner empirical deity" (Edinger).

Shadow: "The inferior (hidden) part of the personality; the sum of all personal and collective psychic elements which, because of their incompatibility with the chosen conscious attitude, are denied expression in life and therefore coalesce into a relatively autonomous 'splinter personality' with contrary tendencies in the unconscious" (Jung).

BIBLIOGRAPHY

Bennet, E. A. *What Jung Really Said*. London: Macdonald, 1966.

Berne, Patricia H., and Savary, Louis M. *Dream Symbol Work*. New York: Paulist Press, 1991.

Chirlot, J. E. *A Dictionary of Symbols*. New York: Philosophical Library, 1962.

Clift, Wallace B. *Jung and Christianity: The Challenge of Reconciliation*. New York: Crossroad Books, 1983.

De Vries, Ad. *Dictionary of Symbols and Imagery*. Amsterdam: Elsevier Science Publishers, 1984.

Edinger, Edward F. *Ego and Archetype: Individuation and the Religious Function of the Psyche*. Baltimore: Penguin, 1973.

————. *The Creation of Consciousness: Jung's Myth for Modern Man*. Toronto: Inner City Books, 1984.

Garfield, Patricia. *Creative Dreaming*. New York: Ballantine (Random House), 1985.

Hall, James A. *Jungian Dream Interpretation: A Handbook of Theory and Practice*. Toronto: Inner City Books, 1983.

————. *Patterns of Dreaming: Jungian Techniques in Theory and Practice*. Boston and London: Shambhala, 1991.

Hunt, Harry T. *The Multiplicity of Dreams: Memory, Imagination, and Consciousness*. New Haven: Yale University Press, 1989.

Johnson, Robert A. *He: Understanding Masculine Psychology*. New York: Harper and Row, 1974.

_____. *Inner Work: Using Dreams & Active Imagination for Personal Growth*. San Francisco: Harper, 1986.

_____. *She: Understanding Feminine Psychology*. New York: Harper and Row, 1976.

Jung, Carl G. *Collected Works*. 20 vols. Bollingen Series XX. Princeton University Press.

_____. *Memories, Dreams, Reflections*. New York: Pantheon Books, 1962.

_____. *Modern Man in Search of a Soul*. New York: Harcourt, Brace & World, 1933.

Kelsey, Morton T. *Dreams: A Way to Listen to God*. New York: Paulist Press, 1978.

_____. *Dreams, God and Revelation: A Christian Interpretation of Dreams*. Minneapolis: Augsburg Publishing House, 1968.

LaBerge, Stephen. *Lucid Dreaming*. Los Angeles: Jeremy Tarcher, 1985.

LeShan, Lawrence. *Alternate Realities: The Search for the Full Human Being*. New York: M. Evans & Co., 1976.

Sanford, John. *Dreams and Healing: A Succinct and Lively Interpretation of Dreams*. New York: Paulist Press, 1978.

_____. *Dreams: God's Forgotten Language*. New York: Lippincott, 1968.

_____. *The Invisible Partners*. New York: Paulist Press, 1980.

Taylor, Jeremy. *Dreamwork: Techniques for Discovering the Creative Power of Dreams*. New York: Paulist Press, 1983.

_____. *Where People Fly and Water Runs Uphill: Using Dreams to Tap the Wisdom of the Unconscious*. New York: Warner Books Inc., 1992.

Von Franz, Marie-Louise. *C. G. Jung: His Myth in Our Time*. London: Hodder & Stoughton, 1975.

————. *The Psychological Meaning of Redemption Motifs in Fairytales.* Toronto: Inner City Books, 1980.

Whitmont, Edward C. *The Symbolic Quest: Basic Concepts of Analytical Psychology* New York: Harper Colophon Books, 1969.

Woodman, Marion. *The Pregnant Virgin: A Process of Psychological Transformation.* Toronto: Inner City Books, 1985.

————. *The Ravaged Bridegroom: Masculinity in Women.* Toronto: Inner City Books, 1990.

WORKSHEET FOR DREAM ANALYSIS

To the reader: We suggest that the worksheet pages that follow be upsized for your own personal use.

Content

1. The Setting:

2. The Images: (objects, animals, people, forms)

3. The Main Theme:

4. The Action or Effect: (Summarize as briefly as possible the movement, energy flow, process, or outcome)

Context

5. The Feeling Tone in the Dream:

6. The Feeling on Waking:

7. Previous Day's Events:

8. Emotional Landscape:
a. What emotional focus was there the day before the dream?

b. What emotionally-charged issues lay ahead?

Associations

9. What associations do you have to any of the images in the dream?

10. What in your life has been similar to elements in the dream?

11. What memories does the dream bring back?

12. What similarities does this dream have to other dreams you've had? To religious or secular stories, legends or fairy tales?

Amplification

13. Balance:
   a. How is this dream different than your waking attitude or values?

   b. What conscious attitude might this dream be trying to balance or compensate?

   c. What does it add to your usual way of living or thinking?

14. Active Imagination: (Go back into the dream and dialogue with any of the people, animals, objects.)
What came out of the dialogue?

15. Gestalt:
   **a. How are you like the persons, animals, objects
      in the dream?**

   **b.(Be that person, animal, object) What does it
      feel like to be that person, etc.?**

**16. Draw or sculpt the dream: What insights or
discoveries came out for you?**

17. Confront your monster: *(If the dream contained a
frightening figure, and if you feel prepared for it, in
active imagination re-enter the dream and approach
the monster, confronting it as you choose. This could
include giving it a name, dialoguing with it or being
more aggressive toward it.)* **Record your findings
below.**

18. What question might this dream be answering?

19. Intervention: *(Invite a religious figure or revered person into the dream scene and see what that person does with the situation)*

20. Completion:
  a. If the dream is incomplete, what ending would you give to it?

  b. If the dream is disturbing to you, what would bring resolution?

21. Archetypal identity: What evidence is there of the presence of transpersonal or archetypal connection in the dream?

22. New Knowledge: What does this dream tell you about yourself and others that you did not know before?

23. Conscious Response: What question, action, or decision do you want to make in response to this dream?

INDEX OF SYMBOLS